WE MUST RE-CIVILIZE AMERICA

DONALD TIVENS

Landmark Publishing, Inc.

Sherman Oaks, California

ISBN: 0-9640631-3-1

DEDICATION

This book is dedicated to my granddaughters, Jessica and Amanda Tivens, who, with the rest of their generation, and their generation's descendants, may inherit an America which is educationally, financially, morally and politically bankrupt.

It is the fervent prayer of the author, that we the people of these United States, through our moral courage, mobilize our efforts to prevent this from ever happening.

ACKNOWLEDGMENTS

To my son, Lynn Tivens, without whose expert word processor techniques, graphic artistry, and diligence to detail, this book many never have been completed.

To my son, Randy Tivens, whose editing and wise counsel were invaluable to this writer.

To Garry Kashuk, an artist extrordinaire, for the book cover.

To Mark Brandes, for my photograph on the back cover.

To W. K. Quarles, for his invaluable research.

TABLE OF CONTENTS

INTRODUCTION

From the time the United States declared its independence from England until the end of World War II, we were a nation which had pride in our many accomplishments. We took a nation of disparate immigrants and molded them into a country which was the envy of the world.

Our schools, our technological accomplishments and our very society was the showcase of what could happen if men and women had common goals of excellence and worked as a people to achieve these goals.

Can our country boast of these qualities today? One just has to turn on the television, or radio, or read any newspaper to see and hear how far we have fallen in the past 50 years, and there does not seem to be any changes in the foreseeable future.

We don't have to relate the statistics of crime to our readers because these killings, rapes, drug operations, drive-by shootings, car-jackings and all of the rest, are a hideous display of where we have come, and nothing but platitudes and tough talk are spoken by our leaders to try to solve our problems.

When the FBI states that Americans can no longer feel safe anywhere, then we as a nation must decide now into which direction we wish to head into the 21st century and beyond. The problems cannot be wished away, and we certainly cannot incarcerate every lawbreaker. There must be another way.

In this book, I will try to illustrate some of the reasons we got to where we are and, if not reversed, the catastrophic direction in which we are heading.

I also will suggest some very important remedies, which may not be the entire solution, but may begin a dialogue to help save our nation for future generations. These remedies are not painless, but change never is. Thomas Jefferson said, *"I hold that a little rebellion, now and then, is a good thing, and as necessary in the political world as storms in the physical."*

We cannot continue with "business as usual" because that would send us over the abyss of national calamity. The crime and education statistics gathered by various agencies are of public record, and a discourse on them is not really necessary as long as it is commonly acknowledged that we no longer travel through the "Emerald City" aboard the "Good Ship Lollipop."

1

THE ERA OF DISRESPECT
AND PERMISSIVENESS

Some future historian is going to look at the last half of the 20th century in the United States and begin to draw a parallel between our nation and the decline and fall of the Roman Empire. He or she will show a decaying of the religious and moral principles along with a lowering of the value of human life.

As many of you have learned in your history books, after the Roman Empire collapsed, the world was plunged into the "dark ages" which lasted for 338 years (476-814 AD), or about the length of time from when the United States was settled to the present.

The great empire which was the first to boast a legislature (the Senate), and which started out to be the first democracy the western world had ever known was eroded from within by corruption, greed, a breakdown of family values and a complete disregard of the magnificent culture it had spawned. No outside armies ever defeated the famed Roman legions. The great empire was vanquished by the breakdown of civilization within its own borders.

When one looks at the United States in the past half-century, the comparison with the Roman empire is chilling, but we had better take stock now, before it is too late. In fact, it may already be too late.

If one needs an example of disrespect, one just needs to turn on a ball game when someone is "singing" the National Anthem. Most of the renditions given in the majority of our professional sporting events are purely disrespectful. For a comparison, just listen to a rendition of "Oh, Canada" whenever the Canadian teams are playing one of our teams, or a rendition of the Mexican or other Latin American anthems when they hold boxing matches in this country, and one can see how far we have slipped.

When the "Star Spangled Banner" was proposed to President Wilson to be our national anthem, he was advised by no less than John Philip Sousa, the great bandmaster. Sousa had conducted the Marine Band for many years before forming his own famous concert band, which traveled worldwide. Sousa wrote out two versions of the "Star Spangled Banner;" one to be played by a band or orchestra, and the other to be sung by a soloist or choir.

These two versions were accepted by an act of Congress in 1931, and they, along with our flag, symbolize The United States of America. Any liberties taken with either of our patriotic symbols can be considered a desecration of the American people.

But why just talk about our national symbols? Just look at the vandalism and graffiti which adorn nearly all freeways and public and private property across our land to see vivid examples of our youth running wild.

When I was a youngster growing up in the 1930s and 1940s, such behavior which was considered "sinful" or "antisocial" and was condemned by society. The perpetrators of those acts were scorned and rebuffed by their peers. These same acts are held up today as examples of people "doing their own thing."

Doing one's own thing has always meant that it was all right to exhibit "eccentric" behavior just as long as it didn't hurt anyone else. This type of thinking has been extrapolated to mean that it is all right to do drugs, become an alcoholic, abuse one's spouse and children and then abandon them so that they may be free to do "their own thing."

A few errant children during the earlier years of the century could be dealt with in our schools or in our criminal justice system. A juvenile delinquent may have been rehabilitated after a brush with the law, or if he had grown into a full criminal, he would be either incarcerated or sent to his death by the courts.

In any case, the number of "misfits" in any particular city or state were, in number, an insignificant minority; and a righteous society was capable of handling these situations.

Today, Los Angeles has an estimated 100,000 gang members and less than 10,000 police to handle these gangs. Society may very well be annihilated by these well-armed and dangerous hoodlums.

Young people from all strata of society have turned to drugs, prostitution, crime and promiscuity as we parents just sit back and shrug our shoulders and wring our hands about the way the youth of this generation have turned bad. We don't seem to want to share in the culpability that we have in contributing to the demise of our society. We are all to blame.

This is not to be taken as an indictment of all parents and all children, because, thankfully, there is still a majority of good families raising good children, only their voices are not the ones being heard. The media seems to sensationalize the rotten apples for the 10:00 news, while the things that are good about us show up in the non prime-time morning shows.

All the while, gratuitous violence and sex show up in our movies and television until we almost believe that we are all a bunch of insensitive animals who thrive on killings, rapes and mayhem. The weird oddities win the day, and normalcy is portrayed as a vice to be merely tolerated. We are in the age of the antihero.

When a movie character such as Rambo is held up as a hero, it is time we begin to examine what we as a society have become, and then take measures to correct our thinking.

When high profile trials such as O. J. Simpson, Rodney King, the Menendez brothers, the bombing of the New York World Trade Center and Oklahoma City take such media attention and almost make folk heroes of the perpetrators of those crimes, which of us can feel safe on our streets, in our homes or work places in the constant fear that some crazed person may decide to get themselves some public attention?

This book is not meant to be a political or religious indictment. It is meant to be an instrument for American preservation. The ensuing chapters will try to illustrate each segment of our problems, and offer proposed solutions.

Let us not forget for a moment that we are at war, and the only way to win this or any other war, is to be diligent in our task, and band together as Americans.

I remember well how Americans mobilized to fight in World War II. The war effort came ahead of personal comforts, new cars, food, household goods — everything. In my opinion, the only way we can save our nation is through a universal effort. The problem belongs to all of us, and only we can solve it.

We have tried, for so long, to perpetuate the status quo, even when we knew much of the status quo was wrong. It is time for us to stand up and defend the things that are right about us, and get rid of what is wrong.

We must take back our streets and neighborhoods from the criminals; we have to get rid of the corrupt politicians who try to be all things to all people merely to get re-elected; we have to educate and civilize our children so that they may represent us as a nation and a society proudly and lastly, we must return America to that wonderful place where every child can have the hope and ambition to grow up and be the best he or she can be.

THE GOVERNMENT

The Constitution of the United States says that the power to govern, raise taxes, fight wars, etc. is vested in We the People. This was meant that the people elect their representatives, legislators and President, and if these elected officials aren't suitable to the electorate, they can be replaced by others who are.

In theory, this sounds like we are the ones who call the shots, but somewhere along the line this idea became sidetracked many times, in many ways and in many places, until the present. Now the laws, rules and regulations are promulgated, written and pushed through by an army of faceless bureaucrats and lobbyists who are neither elected nor appointed by "We the People"— they have become the government, and we had better obey their rules or else.

In the early part of the 20th century, we began to become complacent about our elected officials, and image became more important than substance. In 1921 Warren G. Harding was elected President, in the most part, by women who had the right to vote for the very first time. He was the most handsome of the candidates. Once in office, he permitted his cabinet members and other close cronies to illegally drill oil on government-owned national parks and keep their ill-gotten profits for themselves. The Teapot Dome scandal erupted and some very prominent industrialists were thrown in jail. President Harding was disgraced. He did still manage, however, to bring a mistress into the White House and father an illegitimate child while in office.

But why worry. The country was in the middle of the roaring twenties, there was full employment, the stock market kept setting new records weekly and the world was at peace. Prohibition was the law of the land, but a new breed of bootleggers and gangsters appeared on the scene to provide all of the illegal booze that was wanted for the speakeasies, private clubs and homes. Breaking the law was seen as a legitimate practice, as the song of the day stated, "I Don't Care."

In order to provide an easy circulation of liquor, a network had to be set up to enhance and protect this new lucrative "industry." For this they had to borrow a method from our European ancestry — graft and bribery of police and public officials (those people whom the people elected).

Bootleg gangs developed in those days primarily in the big cities of New York, Philadelphia, Chicago, Detroit, Cleveland and Kansas City mostly in the northeast quadrant of the U.S., which was the most heavily populated and industrialized, and still flourish today and still depend on city hall for their mutual protection.

When prohibition ended, the mob had already gained a foothold in society. By extending their influence into politics, and then later, into labor unions, the mobsters now controlled entire cities, and many legitimate industries.

The novel, and later the motion picture, *The Godfather,* correctly illustrated the insidiousness of an organized crime family, which, on one hand, can fix nearly anything, including setting free a murder suspect, and, on the other hand, send a bunch of henchmen out to eliminate adversaries.

As a native of Chicago, Illinois, I saw how clever politicians manipulated people to vote the party line. They could fix parking or traffic tickets. They could get a driver's license for an individual who couldn't pass the written exam. I even knew of a politician getting an 18 year-old boy off for first degree murder, while his accomplice served 20 years to life.

The incident involved two teenagers who robbed an elderly shoemaker and tied him up while they took money and ransacked his shop. The man died while the crime was being committed, making it a first degree murder.

Both boys were caught by the police and arrested. The father of one of the boys came from a large family, all of whom had several children.

The father of that boy went to plead with his alderman, who was a neighbor of mine, and only lived a few doors away from the family in question. The weight of justice was left up to the discretion of the politician.

He didn't see a father with an errant son, rather he calculated how many votes he would "own" for the next election, just from the adults in the boy's family, and then, how many additional votes he could anticipate in the future, with such a prolific family.

The rest was simple. He made a couple of phone calls to policemen and judges, then went into the jail and took out the man's son.

This is one instance which I personally witnessed. How many other "fixings" transpired in Chicago, Detroit, St. Louis, Cleveland and New York is hard to calculate, but suffice it to say that machine politicians welcomed these kinds of situations so that they could help the little people and then, forevermore, control their allegiance for whomever they wished to elect.

But all of this fixing had a very heavy price. These benevolent politicians now owned not only the individuals they helped, but also had the adulation of the rest of the families and circles of friends of those people so helped. This fixing and helping bought votes on election day.

We were no longer concerned about the qualifications of the candidates, rather we were expected to vote for the party slate. For many years we would hear that winning of the Democratic primary in Chicago was "tantamount to election."

Machine politics in cities like New York, Boston, Cleveland and Detroit have given people a very cynical attitude regarding their leaders. To bring this idea into better focus, I have invented the fictional Johnson family.

Mrs. Johnson is a world-class commercial baker of bread, pies, cakes and sweet rolls. She, her husband and their two grown sons decide to leave their small town in Nebraska and try their luck in the big city of Chicago.

They use their life savings to purchase a bankrupt bakery, which is equipped with ovens, refrigerators, baking equipment and two nearly-new delivery trucks.

Mr. Johnson worked for many years as a bakery route salesman, and he would be the one to secure the restaurant, hotel and other commercial accounts. The sons, both in their 20s, would deliver the merchandise to the accounts set up by their father.

What I have described is a family-owned business. No outside help is required and all of the work is performed by the four family members. They don't have to join any unions because they are all self-employed principals, outside of a business license and resale permit, no other legal documents are required of them.

On day one, the two young men get into their trucks and begin to deliver their baked goods. How far do you think they will go before one or both of the trucks will get flat tires?

On day two, one or both of them may have an accident with another truck. And by day three, if they persist, one of the young men may be found floating in the Chicago River with a bullet in his head. If you are not wired in with the powers that be, you just can't do business in Chicago.

Now, if you can't drive a pastry truck safely down Chicago streets without playing ball with the boys, then tell me how you could be elected to Congress, as Mayor, Alderman or even Dog Catcher? The answer is, you *can't*.

Protection Racket

Back in the 1930s and 40s, the organized crime bosses and their gangster underlings needed to use muscle to get their way. The protection racket was depicted in the movies of the 30s and 40s with dramatic uses of force. The typical lines that were said to business owners were, to the effect, if you don't pay up, you will have a broken window, or a mysterious fire or any number of other threats.

These types of scenarios in the genre of gangster movies made for good drama; however, the real way the protection racket has been run is in a very different way, without the threats.

For example, when a person wanted to start up a restaurant in one of the large northeastern cities, he would have to get a zoning permit. This zoning had to be approved by the city, which, in fact, is run by the local politicians. They would only grant the zoning to the restaurant operator if he agreed to purchase his meat, vegetables, bakery goods, liquor, and laundry, from specified suppliers, who were on the approved list of the politicians.

Once the arrangement was agreed upon, the restaurant was not only given the zoning approval, but the restaurant owner was guaranteed protection from any competitive restaurants specializing in the same type of food within a prescribed area. Very often the protection could encompass one or two square miles. Other would-be competitors were kept out of the protected area.

By controlling the zoning, the politicians, union bosses and their several vendors (who undoubtedly kicked-back a share of their earnings), have had a stranglehold on much of the commerce inside of their jurisdiction.

This same type of protection arrangement works with nearly every type of retail business, and the payoffs are substantial. These clever political bosses do not have to resort to violence; they merely control their cities through "legal" means.

I left Chicago in 1947 and have been back on visits every year or two since, but I can still name many major restaurants in that city because they have remained stationary all of these years. Some of these businesses are run by the children and grandchildren of the original owners, but some of the scenario continues just as it did 50 years ago.

I remember the cop on the beat in my neighborhood. He lived in the same apartment house in which we resided. He was a bachelor who shared the apartment with his widowed mother and divorced sister. He was a very quiet-spoken chap who went about his rounds and didn't speak to anyone unless he was spoken to. He was a foot patrolman whose beat was our neighborhood.

In the morning, he would leave the apartment dressed in his blue uniform, like any Chicago cop, and was armed with a gun and a billy club. I would watch him head for the cigar store located under the "El" platform a block away.

This was a very unusual cigar store, mainly because they didn't sell enough cigars, cigarettes, candy or ice cream to keep a chicken alive. The "real business" was in the back room.

This cozy back room had a racing wire, a couple of tables for poker and other illegal gambling and book-making activities. After an hour or so, the officer would reappear and walk his beat for half a mile south to the local pool hall, also equipped with the same "back room" as the cigar store, but with the added attractions of slot machines and a roulette wheel.

His last major stop was a very unique barber shop. The space for cutting hair only took up the front of the store. The rest of the very large building was also a very important bookmaking and gambling operation.

After making those three calls, it was time for him to quit for the day. My neighbor, the officer, retired a mil-lionaire. I met him quite by accident many years later in Phoenix, and he introduced me to his new wife. They had recently purchased a large home in Scottsdale, a very fashionable new upscale community, and I was invited to be their guest. I never took them up on the invitation.

A couple of very important things can be learned from my personal experiences. Firstly, if an ordinary officer on the beat (who earned $1,000 — $1,500 per year in the 1940s) can retire in style through payoffs, what kind of graft goes on in the higher strata? Secondly, it is very interesting that this individual, along with many others I learned of in later years, made it their business to keep a low financial profile at home, where they were known, but later were able to be anonymous thousands of miles away, where they could live lavishly off their graft.

Freeways and Tollways

The strangest phenomena of the big machine and crooked politics is the attitude of the very people effected by these political machines. They do not believe that they are adversely effected, so why should they make waves?

This was the same reasoning a majority of the Italian people used in regards to their 1940s dictator, Benito Mussolini. The trains ran on time, the streets were clean so they saw nothing wrong with their kind dictator.

Let me illustrate a point when most people in the urban areas in the northeastern part of this country had been unjustly treated by these "benevolent" political bosses.

In 1952, President Eisenhower and the United States Congress passed the National Defense Highway Act, which allotted $42 billion dollars for 42,000 miles of freeways across the lower 48 states. The money would come from gasoline taxes, a tax that was added to the cost of each gallon purchased.

The formula was to be based roughly on a 90% to 95% contribution by the Federal Government, the rest coming from the states. We can identify these freeways built by the little blue shields with white numbers placed along the right-of-way of each federally-funded freeway.

One would rightly ask, so what's wrong with that? How can politicians get rich off of that kind of program?

Those people who live in the northeast corridor of this nation have, in addition to the freeways, many tollways. When we look at places such as California, Texas, Arizona, Nevada and many other states which have many thousands of miles of freeways, isn't it unusual that urban areas with far fewer miles of highways need to have tollways, where a driver must feed the kitty every few miles with pocket change?

The reason for the great disparity in freeways verses tollways is that when the rights-of-way for these projects were acquired in the locales where machine politicians controlled the areas, the people whose properties were condemned by eminent domain actions by the local cities and states, could not sell their properties to the freeway authorities for the price that was set in the condemnation proceedings. They had to sell their properties to one or more of the appointed representatives of the politicians.

The politicians then jacked-up the prices substantially, and sold these highly over-inflated parcels to the freeway authorities. Through this practice, some politicians became instant multimillionaires, and the freeway project thus assaulted, ran out of money.

The only way, therefore, to finish the rest of the freeway miles required was for the States to set up a bonding authority, in order to build tollways.

How does this effect the citizens? They wind up paying for the highways twice!

When we look at the cost overruns of public buildings, garbage collection, military acquisitions and a list of products and services longer than this writing would permit, is it any wonder that those "nice people" we elected to public office, or those benevolent civil servants, come away from government fabulously wealthy?

Money is sent to offshore banks to avoid Federal taxes and all the watchdogs in the world will never find a penny.

If I, as a youngster growing up in Chicago, could observe these and so many other incidents of political graft and corruption, how many other people, not only in Chicago, but throughout the United States, have witnessed similar, and worse, instances in their own towns, cities, counties and states? In fact, it is amazing that more is not exposed in the media of the road our leaders walk in order to get to the top.

How can we expect honesty and forthright dealing from our citizens if our leaders are crooked? Is it O.K. to cheat on your income taxes? Can you read off of the exam paper of the genius sitting next to you so that you might secure a higher grade?

When is it O.K. to cheat, lie, steal, take unfair advantage, rape, molest or kill? Where do you draw the line? Is it all right to do these things when you are far from home, when you can be sure nobody is watching? Is the honor code at West Point, Annapolis, and throughout our entire education system, just for suckers?

If it is O.K. for former President Nixon to cover up an illegal act; or for former Vice President Agnew to resign rather than face racketeering charges; or for senators and congressmen to spend hot checks at the Congressional Post Office; or for many federal, state and local legislators to not go to prison for influence peddling and graft, then why should any of us obey any laws? Do you think that we have uncovered all of the crooks in politics just because a few of their number were caught and thrown into prison, or forced to resign?

A few years ago I took a cruise to a Caribbean island and joined a tour around that island. When the bus tour passed a hill with a large, sprawling mansion and grounds covering the hill, the driver said to us, "Do you remember Senator so-and-so from Massachusetts?" I said to him, "not bad for $40,000 a year (which is what the good senator earned those years, legally)."

The late President Lyndon Johnson was elected to Congress in the 1930s, during the heart of the depression. He had been a school teacher, and he and his wife both came from a middle-class background. By the time he assumed the Presidency after the assassination of John F. Kennedy, Johnson had amassed a fortune. He owned the LBJ Ranch in Texas, a radio station and who knows what else, all of this on the earnings of a Congressman, a Senator and later the Vice President. The man somewhere became a multimillionaire, and nobody yelled foul.

President John F. Kennedy started the "New Frontier" and Lyndon Johnson called his program The Great Society. Both programs began affirmative action, mega-welfare, food-stamps and a whole host of giveaway programs, none of which, most of our citizens wanted or could afford.

These socialistic programs of wealth redistribution has cost our taxpayers dearly. According to a recent speech by William F. Buckley, which I attended, welfare has cost our people over $3 trillion dollars since the 1960s and things are worse than ever.

The director of the National Health Care Anti-Fraud Association estimated that "as much as $30 billion tax dollars were consumed by fraud."

This whole idea of wealth redistribution has gotten out-of-control. The subsidies on Section 8 Housing sponsored by Housing and Urban Development will cost taxpayers over $37 billion this year, according to the House Subcommittee on Employment.

When I was a young man, I was told by my elders that there is no free lunch. With these social programs, not only is there free lunch, but there are also free groceries, housing, cash money, with which some people purchase liquor, drugs and a whole host of goodies, none of which are monitored very well, by anyone.

A major segment of our society are ambitious, hardworking, God-loving and educated men and women; and they are required to pay ever-increasing taxes to support the indolent, able bodied dropouts of society.

Not only is this manifestly unfair, but as people get in the habit of being on the dole, they want and expect even more and more each year in the way of material help.

This has got to stop, and stop soon!

In this day of *the image*, it is of utmost importance that we forget about our personal comfort and begin to insist on honest leaders who tell the truth and do not promise to be everything to everybody just to get elected. Before the 1992 election, I heard that a U.S. Senator must raise $6,000 dollars per day, 365 days per year (including Sunday's and Holidays, etc.) just so they might have a big enough financial war chest for the next election, six years later. In their zeal to raise this money, the Senator must ally himself with many special interest groups, whose agendas may not agree with his or her philosophy, but whose money will help to get him or her elected.

Is it any wonder that "We the People" don't count nearly as much as big money influence-peddlers? Why do you think they are putting out the *large donations* — because they believe in the candidates?

"To the victor go the spoils." This old political maxim means that the elected President, Governor, Senator and so on could appoint their good friends, relatives and political supporters to cabinet positions, ambassadorships and department heads. All of this was under the heading of political rewarding for loyalty. It wasn't a big deal until the income tax was voted into law in 1913.

At first there wasn't very much tax money involved; therefore political mischief was rather limited to handing out the glory to close associates.

It wasn't until the government, under Franklin Roosevelt, began to get into the business of business that we began to see untold power and financial abuses. The gamesmanship of budgets and waste became the by-product of the Federal Government, the States and cities who learned the game, by imitating Washington.

According to the American Association of Home Builders, new housing in the United States is adversely impacted by rules and regulations in the amount of 45% of all cost. By the time a builder gets through an environmental impact report (which could take as long as two years), red tape at all levels of agencies add on the high costs of finance and property taxes, this could break all but the financially strongest of developers. A project from the outset until homes are available for sale can take from three to five years.

If consumers were told up front that the promulgation of all of these fancy laws make a $65,000 home cost $100,000; or a $130,000 home cost $200,000 how do you think they would vote?

The workings of government at *all* levels mostly has been to pad their agencies with as many personnel as they can, and then have each agency ask for more and more budget money each year.

It is estimated that at least two-thirds of the money appropriated for welfare and other social subsidies, are eaten up by salaries and other bureaucratic overhead.

My proposal to reduce high cost of *needed* social programs would be to take the budgeted money away from the Federal agencies and let these funds be administered by private agencies such as the YMCA, Salvation Army, American Red Cross, United Way/Red Feather, Boys/Girls Clubs of America, Boys/Girls Scouts of America, Big Brother and Big Sisters organizations and other legitimate national service organizations like these who not only have long and respected track records, but who for the most part, have overhead in the 10% — 15% ranges.

These and other charitable organizations use a great deal of volunteer support and they are forced to spend a great deal of time and money in fund raising efforts.

The present mood of Congress is to take the funds for welfare and other social programs and give block grants to the states. I am very much opposed to that idea because we would merely be shifting the whole mess from one set of bureaucrats to another set of bureaucrats. The overhead would still be too high and money appropriated for the truly needy people would be diminished just as it has, the past thirty plus years, by salaries, perks and the rest of the high administrative cost.

My proposal would need only a fraction of the administrative costs that we presently have and money would be distributed at the local and neighborhood level by local people who are familiar with the needs and problems of their less-fortunate brethren.

In the case of housing, automobiles and many other consumer products, the consumer not only pays these costs which are passed on, but they also must support the agencies of government through their sales taxes. In other words, we must pay twice for the same product.

Is it any wonder that hundreds of thousands of businesses and jobs have relocated out of this country?

Our leaders keep talking about small business being the backbone of America, and then they pass punitive taxes and laws to break the backbone of the backbone.

I have spoken to many business owners over the last 30 years and have heard them recite all of their grievances against our big, insensitive government. The Libertarian Party has had as its platform for many years to just chop these government bureaus and agencies off with a meat ax, rather than phasing them out using sunset laws and other means.

The morale in the business community is at an all-time low. Writing to one's Congressional representative doesn't do any good because it is those representatives

who set up this unwieldy behemoth. So what do we do
— revolt?

The real answer is that we must take back our government through the ballot box. The idea that less than
50% of the eligible voters voted in the 1992 Presidential
election (Clinton received only 42% of the actual vote)
is a sad commentary on our free nation.

John Dewey said, "We naturally associate democracy
with freedom of action, but freedom of action without
freed capacity of thought behind it is only chaos." In
other words, we will only get the kind of government we
deserve; that translates to voting for the right candidate,
not the party line. Party machine politics has brought us
to where we are, and we will sink further until we vote
for candidates who display freedom of action, willing-
ness to advance America (not their own candidacy), and
lead us into the 21st century with plans to regain our
former prominence. Anything less is not acceptable.

The way the free enterprise system in this country
was setup to be abolished, one segment at a time, will be
a treatise for some future economist to point out. The
government's execution of neo-socialism has been a program of divide and conquer by using the police powers
of a strong central government.

Many small towns and cities, particularly in the
Northeastern section of our nation, are destitute because
industrial companies and factories which employed most
of the town's workers have either gone bankrupt, or were
forced to leave the country because of regulations, taxes
and the prohibitive cost of doing business.

Our government succeeded in destroying, or chasing away many of our manufacturers and then turned to other industries such as construction, real estate, banking, retail department stores, and the list goes on. The last bastion of free enterprise, the medical profession, is the latest to be under attack.

The socialist philosophy involves bringing everyone in society down to the same level, and then allowing Big Brother to set the prices, products, wages, services, and everything else in peoples lives.

This whole over-budgeted, top-heavy, money-wasting business that our Federal, State, County, and City governments have become is a very cruel and treacherous method of assuming power. They then perpetuate that power through clever manipulation of the media and the party faithful. In some places it is called machine politics, in others, merely control of our income, taxes, property, schools, jobs, and our very lives.

The power to tax is unlimited, and so is the control it gives to politicians, bureaus, agencies, and their legions of employees.

In this century we fought four wars; World War I, World War II, Korea, and Viet Nam; plus three police actions, or whatever the fancy name given at the time. Grenada, Desert Storm, and Haiti, and at this writing, we are going into the former war-ravaged Yugoslavia.

The American people saw justification for World Wars I and II, and backed the White House and Congress to the hilt by purchasing bonds, doing war work, putting up with shortages of consumer goods, and giving up our young men to the cause of world freedom.

The reason given for getting into the Korean and Vietnam Wars were a lot more fuzzy compared to the previous goals. In Korea, we weren't supposed to win the war, but just lose hundreds of thousands of American lives to keep the "Communists" north of an arbitrary latitude which some politicians had drawn on a map.

This caused many of our young people, both in and out of service, to rebel against their own government and our nation's institutions. This, in my opinion, was the beginning of the end of the practice of raising a generation of young people who were disciplined, ambitious, and studious.

The emergence of people like James Dean the Rebel Without a Cause and Elvis Presley soon became the rallying forces for the anti-establishment beliefs, music, dress, and attitude of a generation.

Young people no longer had faith in our government, and they showed their revulsion through antisocial actions. Drug and liquor usage began to increase greatly by young people, and young people's social, academic, and job habits began to decline in quality.

When the Vietnam War began, a whole new generation of young people just "dropped out" of our American culture. School dropouts were commonplace; youngsters who came from the most affluent families of our society began to share in an underground society, the core of which was rebellion against the perceived establishment.

Drugs, liquor, dress codes, loud music, and a rapid decline of morality were the hallmarks of the "beat generation" of the 60s and early 70s. Our jails and prisons became loaded with young kids from "good families," and the more we talked and wrote about these problems, the less we were heard.

Young people dying because of overdoses became commonplace, and the illegitimate birth rate became an important statistical factor.

The government turned deaf ears to the pleas of their own people during both the Korean and Vietnamese conflicts to the point that they were forced to put down local insurrections with armed government troops, such as what happened at Kent State in Ohio, and many hundreds of other less publicized riots.

Then, in a move just as uncertain as the one of going into Vietnam with a military action, we decided to pull out and let the Vietnamese unify their country.

The cost monetarily is the smallest price paid of these two wars. What these two wars really cost our nation was credibility in our President and Congress. Our young people saw no hope for themselves when they saw their innocent peers being conscripted into no-win, no-goal wars, which cost countless thousands of people their lives and limbs, just because the government thought it was time to have a war, the younger generation turned off toward society.

Brian Lamb, CEO of C-SPAN, worked under the Assistant Secretary of Defense for Public Affairs, Arthur Sylvester, who was quoted early in the Kennedy administration as saying that the government had a right to lie. Lamb said that "... it was my first education into how news was made."

A good many of these young people from the Korean and Vietnam conflict eras are the very ones who have caused the terrible statistics of family breakups, misfit children, crime, drugs, and all of the rest of the horrible social problems plaguing us today.

We cannot turn back the clock and undo all of the harm that was done to our nation in those wars, plus the so-called police actions in Grenada, Desert Storm, and Haiti, but we can at the very least elect leaders who do not visualize America as the policeman of the world.

There is already saber-rattling rhetoric in Congress today relating to going into the former Yugoslavia to settle that civil war mess. The several ethnic groups that make up that embattled nation have been warring with each other for centuries. We don't have either the money or the will power, as a nation to go in and settle this or any other feuds between nations.

We should be fully aware of the bloodshed and human rights violations that are going on, but it is not our problem, and we have no business sticking our noses into other's conflicts.

If we are going to "Re-Civilize America," one of our most important priorities is to show our young people that we, as a nation, use civilized methods in our dealings of problems within our nation, and in our relationships with other nations.

If we try to impress upon our youth that the use of force is barbarian and antiquated, and then we send our Air Force, Navy, Army, or Marines after our adversaries, what message are we delivering?

If we are going to try to "Re-Civilize America," we must begin at the top in order to provide role models for our citizens. Politics and taxing as usual must no longer be the order of the day.

We must get rid of machine politics and make our elected officials accountable to their constituents.

> *Power tends to corrupt and*
> *absolute power corrupts absolutely.*
> *—John Dalber Acton (1834–1902)*

TAXES

The Constitution of the United States Ratified 1787 Section 9, Article 4 states:

"No taxation, or other direct tax shall be laid, unless in proportion to the census or enumeration herein before directed to be taken." In other words — no income tax would be allowed.

Amendment XVI, Ratified February 25, 1913 states:

"The Congress shall have power to lay and collect taxes in income, from whatever source derived, without apportionment among the several States, and without regard to any census or enumeration."

The founding fathers of our nation, in their great wisdom, saw the terrible dangers inherent in a direct income tax. The point in Section 9, Article 4 ,was argued and discussed at great length. The final form was not an arbitrary point just thrown into the Constitution because it sounded like a good idea.

These great thinkers were worried about a strong central government located many miles away from the rank-and-file population.

John Marshall, a chief Justice of the U.S. Supreme Court said, in 1819, "The power to tax involves the power to destroy."

It has long been my observation that the way our Federal and State governments levy taxes is too costly, too burdensome, and too unfair. Income taxes require very large and sophisticated collection and administrative bureaus.

The laws of the United States and the 50 individual State governments are extremely specific regarding monetary judgments against individuals and corporations. Before a judgment for money or property is permitted, there must be a court hearing in front of a judge, where both sides are permitted to bring in evidence, witnesses, and any other pertinent information to aid the court, such as case laws, precedents, and experts in the field.

Only after the court finds for the plaintiff does the judge execute a ruling against the defendant. This briefly is what is known as due process of law. The defendant can be represented by an attorney, and is able to defend his position before any action is taken against him.

The way the Internal Revenue Services works is in complete contradiction to the Constitution. A single agent can take it upon himself to file tax liens against a taxpayer, bank accounts, real estate, automobiles, and other personal property which can be seized, and the taxpayer never has his day in court to defend himself.

The Internal Revenue Service is judge, jury, and executioner, and there is no legal defense against their actions unless they go to tax court and spend untold sums of money. I have known people who have had heart attacks, strokes and other debilitating illnesses as consequences of the acts of the Internal Revenue Service.

Judges and Lawyers

One of the reasons it has been so difficult to declare the income tax laws unconstitutional is that the judges who hear the cases are paid by those income taxes. In other words, we are asking these judges to fire themselves.

In recent years, the F.B.I. has executed many sting operations against judges and lawyers who were accepting bribes on cases they were trying. A number of these people were sent to jail after they were found guilty.

It is my opinion that the legislators, judges, lawyers, and civil officials who have been investigated and brought to justice is only just the tip of the iceberg. There are people in high places that have many slick and contrived means by which they can accept bribes and never be caught.

I heard of one case where a powerful legislator was approached by a group of business people asking for him to support legislation in which they had a vested interest. The legislator suggested that this group retain his law firm, at a fee of $50,000 per year for three years, and then he would guarantee that their law would pass.

In this instance, it would be impossible to trace the $150,000 paid to this legislator.

The payola to legislators which winds up in offshore banks is legend. Usually the accounts are in the names of family members or friends, and are all but impossible to trace.

We cannot legislate honesty, but we can keep politicians from getting a long-term foothold by limiting the time they spend in office. The same holds for judges or prosecuting attorneys, who are in positions to be able to fix most crimes. These people must also have limited terms so that they do not continue to make the criminal justice system the mockery that it is.

I do not believe that the framers of our Constitution had this type of high-handed ruthlessness in mind when they planned the form our Republic was to take. In fact, they guarded against just such an eventuality, in the Bill of Rights.

This kind of disregard of people's rights is derived from totalitarian governments which we have witnessed in this century. There were no human or property rights in Hitler's Germany, Stalin's Soviet Union, or the present People's Republic of China.

Our people are terrorized and intimidated by an agency of government which is supported by us through our taxes. This agency has gone too far in its zeal to achieve the impossible monetary goals which are required to support an unwieldy, top-heavy, and irrelevant Federal bureaucracy.

This whole crazy nightmare belongs to another time and another place. The America of tomorrow is going to have to be more self-reliant, and free of government intervention. The taxes needed to support such a leaner government are going to have to be more fairly paid by everyone.

By eliminating the Internal Revenue Service I would like to see the government switch to a value added tax, or what I like to call a "point of sale" tax. This tax would be paid by everyone. We wouldn't have to worry about real or imagined tax evaders. If one must eat, pay rent, drive a car, purchase clothing, visit the doctor or dentist, and make all of the rest of normal daily purchases, one would pay a proportional share of taxes. These taxes could be collected and administered by the same agencies in each city and state which presently collect sales taxes.

A simple formula for a tax rate could be arrived at through which each entity, (Federal, State, County, and City) would receive its fair share.

No more liens on property or other ruthless methods would be needed. We never hear of "crackdowns" on citizens who don't pay their sales taxes! The value-added or point of sale tax would just be another sales tax.

There has been much talk about a flat rate income tax. This would not work because the same cheaters who presently do not pay income tax would continue *not* paying a flat tax.

I have heard estimates of as much as 30% or 40% of gainfully employed people who never report income, or pay any income tax. The point of sale tax would *force* these cheaters to pay their fair share if they wanted any goods and services.

Unfortunately, because of ever-increasing income tax rates, the people and their own State and Federal governments have become adversaries. The tax collector has taken on the image of the Gestapo as it existed in Hitler's Germany. The tax payer is considered guilty until *he* proves his innocence.

This has caused otherwise good, hardworking people to figure out schemes to cheat their country out of their money. Once this whole income tax machine went into motion, the cause of freedom in our nation was dealt a severe blow.

Not only have most people disliked the collection of their hard-earned money based on some arbitrary tax rates which never stay the same each year, they also dislike being lied to by their President and Congress whenever the subject of taxes comes up.

The most compelling reason to do away with the income tax is that every person does not share in the tax. When you think of the thousands of day-laborers in households across America, plus the gardeners, the industrial day people who collect their wages in cash (under the table), the millions of small Mom and Pop restaurants, video stores, motels, and (the list in endless) the many others who report little or no income tax, but who are able to live in nice homes and drive new automobiles then you have to agree that the income tax method is patently unfair.

People who go on welfare and still work in a "cash" world are being given a free ride at the expense of those of us unfortunate enough to be salaried, or who are in businesses that require bank records and other transactions which can be easily traced.

I have witnessed people purchasing big ticket items such as automobiles, appliances, and real estate, and they never make a down payment or monthly payment with a check. They either used cash or money orders.

A few years ago, the U.S. Treasury Department tried to figure out how much money there was in circulation both in the United States and in foreign countries. They found out that there were many billions of dollars unaccounted for. It is my opinion that many of these billions of dollars are stashed away in safety deposit boxes, off shore banks and kept hidden in peoples homes, and the tax collectors are none the wiser.

These and thousands of other reasons too numerous to mention cause the legitimate, taxpaying citizens grounds to question why they shouldn't also go "underground" and avoid paying income taxes.

All of us have seen young, clean-cut, able-bodied people spend thousands of dollars in food stamps and then take their groceries away in late model luxury cars. It is a daily happening, and meanwhile we are asked to raise our children, to be honest, forthright citizens. The blatant contradictory abuses are too obvious.

I have already discussed the idea that power corrupts, and so does unequal treatment have a corrupting influence on all Americans, young and old. Therefore unfair and unjust income tax method must be done away with.

Congress tried to debate an add-on sales tax in 1993, but the way the tax was proposed, it made no sense and was doomed to failure. Surprise!, Surprise!

Congress is only too happy to keep business going as usual. Why should they try to change to an honest system?

Therefore, they proposed an add-on tax which would be separately placed on the raw material, the finished product, and finally the retail sale. This would mean three separate and distinct taxes on the very same product. How could any fair-minded person buy that idea? The answer was, they couldn't and wouldn't. Therefore, they thought why don't we just keep it like it is? They took a simple problem, and in true Washington fashion, they made the solution so complex that even a sophisticated computer couldn't make sense of their answers.

The simple solution is a retail tax on all *finished* goods. The percentage may be anywhere from 5% to 15%, depending upon our nations needs, and with this type of tax, everyone would have to pay. We don't have to label the tax as "income tax;" we could call it a "point-of-sale tax." This way, every person in the nation would have to pay a share of running the government.

The cost of collecting, administering, and enforcing income taxes could be eliminated, at a tremendous savings, and everyone would be treated and taxed equally. One big savings would be the time and money spent on accountants and tax experts.

One of the arguments against a consumer tax is that the poor person gets taxed as much as the rich person. This argument doesn't hold water in practice, because

35

the rich person spends a great deal more money on goods and services than the poor person, and would therefore pay a higher amount of taxes each year.

This point-of-sale tax is the only way we can provide a level playing field for everyone. The person who spends $500 per month would pay $25-50 in taxes based on a 5 — 10 percentage rate. The person who spends $4,000 per month would pay $200-$400 in taxes. Richer people would pay more in taxes, but most importantly, *everyone* would be paying.

States which have income taxes could then impose another 1% to 3% over the Federal tax, but the overall effect would remain the same.

If everyone pays a share of taxes, instead of the present "catch me if you can" system, then we would be able to hold our heads up and proclaim that we are giving our citizens a *fair proposition.*

We could eliminate the need for the Internal Revenue Service, and use the mechanisms the states already use to collect sales taxes. The entire distribution could be reduced to a formula based on percentages to each municipality, just as cities and states do now. The cost of collecting taxes at both the federal and state levels could be eliminated, and more importantly, Americans could feel like a "free people" once again.

The April madness is both financially and psychologically debilitating, and a simple pay-as-you spend tax method would cause everyone to contribute according to their abilities, without the pressures of proving one's innocence.

*When there is an income tax, the just man will pay
more and the unjust less on the same amount of income.*
—Plato (428–348 BC)

WHAT THE "NEW FRONTIER," "GREAT SOCIETY," AND OTHER "NEO-SOCIALIST" PROGRAMS HAVE COST OUR COUNTRY

We will never be able to convince the American people that we as a nation are not greedy and power-hungry unless we return the cost of running the government to within reasonable and prudent bounds.

Money gets appropriated each year to government agencies because they have received money for the past 20 or 30 years, and they are also given a cost of living adjustment each year because their employees' unions have this item written into their contracts.

Political patronage traditions continue with cabinet and department head appointments granted almost daily. The money-eating machine continues to grow and become bigger than the nation that feeds it.

We have a cabinet level Department of Education which boasts having one staff member for every school district in the nation. Money continues to be appropriated each year with incremental raises, and still, Johnny and Mary can't read, write, or perform simple arithmetic problems — yet we have a Department of Education that shuffles papers and spends money.

When will we put our heads out the window as Peter Finch did in the movie *Network* and say, "I am as mad as hell and I won't take it any longer?"

In the 1992 California senatorial election Bruce Herschensohn, a candidate for the Senate and a former aide to President Nixon, stated that the Federal Government receives $4 billion dollars per year for education from the taxpayers in California, and returns only $3 billion to the state. And the money they do return to the state has more strings on it than Pinocchio.

Not only does this involve a lot of foolish duplication, but it is at a tremendous cost of lowering of educational standards. (More about education in a later chapter.)

It may have sounded like a high-minded enterprise to have a Federal Department of Education, but the concept has failed. Instead of folding the department, however, the taxpayers were told to raise the ante in hopes of making the Department of Education work — forget about it! Twenty years with no results is long enough.

We have a Department of Transportation which is in charge of our roads, highway, bridges, waterways, air traffic, and so on. After 20 years, do we have better roads?

Freeways? Bridges? The way we continue to budget, you would think the Department of Transportation is doing a world class job. Wrong! Much of the money gets eaten up in salaries, perks, retirement, pensions, and once in a while a freeway gets repaired or a new bridge built, but who asks questions? As long as everyone plays the game by the rules, the game will go on.

Abraham Lincoln once said, "You can fool all of the people some of the time, you can fool some of the people all of the time, but you can not fool all of the people all of the time."

I believe that the American people are fed up with being fooled by an impersonal, selfish, arrogant, and corrupt oligarchy, and if given an alternate solution, might elect a slate of legislators who will comply with our wishes for having an efficient running government..

I am not forgetting about the waste that goes on at the state and city levels. The problem of waste and mismanagement is universal. We have given our leaders a blank checkbook and they have run wild. It is as much our fault as it is theirs, and only we can solve this situation. We must do away with these departments by making them all subject to sunset laws; eg., each agency must justify its existence before an unbiased panel of experts in the field, along with an equal number of concerned, knowledgeable citizens. If, say, the Department of Education cannot justify its existence, it would then be phased out.

The preposterous idea of continually funding counterproductive agencies or other functions of government just because they have existed for so many years is an idea which has caused much of our current financial dilemma.

Many years ago, Ford Motor Company developed a new automobile which they called the "Edsel." They set up an entire dealer network throughout the U.S., and in some foreign countries, and they advertised and promoted the new auto for several years.

The product just didn't have the consumer demand, so after several very expensive years, Ford Motor Company dropped the Edsel and counted their losses.

If the Edsel was a government product, it would still be produced and marketed, whether it had consumer acceptance or not. This is the primitive way the government agencies have been run for years.

These agencies hire staff for career positions, and many of the people serve 20, 30, 40 years with salaries, vacations with pay, world-class medical insurance, and retirement pensions which are far superior to anything private industry can offer, and all at the expense of us unsuspecting taxpayers.

The following chart illustrates how our Congressional legislators have been spending our hard-earned money. Blue ribbon groups such as the Grace Commission and other prestigious think tanks have, for years, been telling us that the waste and mismanagement of our economy has put us into the $5 trillion dollar national debt we now face.

For many years, I have heard the apologists for this welfare state say that we are a rich country. If we were indeed rich, we wouldn't be in debt to the tune of $5 trillion dollars.

It is estimated that salaries, overhead, rents, etc., account for from 60% to 80% of the numbers shown on this chart. For instance, the Education Department budget is nearly all salaries and overhead, and for the eight years illustrated, the budget went from $16,800 billion dollars to $30,414 billion dollars, 81% increase.

In similar fashion, the food stamp program more than doubled from $12,405 billion to $25,549 billion.

The health and human services (not including social security, which is an off-budget item) went from a whopping $148,893 billion to a staggering $278,901 billion, nearly doubling in eight years.

I have added up the columns of the departments' spending illustrated in the chart, and then entered the budget deficit for each year.

If these departments were eliminated and their costs stricken from the budget, we could not only show a surplus each year, we would be able to begin reducing the national debt.

This would sound like a simple game of 4th grade arithmetic when we just look at the raw numbers. Unfortunately, the liberal Congress, who owe their jobs to the freeloaders in our society, puts out a blitz of media and mail propaganda to these people on the dole, and use histrionics so that they aren't defeated by candidates who wish to reform the system. You can just imagine the threats and coercion hurled by the bureaucrats and their families in the departments about to be phased out.

The proposition I am explaining is very simple. Are we going to continue to have a nation where the gainfully employed, tax paying citizens must continue to

In Millions

PROGRAM	1987	1988	1989	1990	1991	1992	1993	1994
Food Stamps	$12,405	13,145	13,725	15,923	19,649	22,800	24,602	25,549
Farmers Home Administration	3,749	7,277	7,608	6,713	6,629	4,455	2,042	1,880
Education Dept.	16,800	18,246	21,608	23,109	25,339	26,047	30,414	24,699
Energy	10,688	11,166	11,387	12,023	12,459	15,439	16,801	17,839
Health & Human Services (No Soc. Sec.)	148,893	158,991	172,301	193,679	217,969	257,961	282,774	278,901
Housing & Urban Development	15,464	18,956	19,680	20,187	22,751	24,470	25,185	25,845
Transportation Minus Fed. Avation Admin.	20,536	21,212	20,867	22,246	23,262	24,405	25,657	23,495
Totals	228,535	248,993	267,173	293,880	328,058	375,577	407,475	398,208
Budget Deficit for each year	-149,661	-155,151	-153,319	-220,388	-269,492	-290,204	-254,948	-203,200

support those people who are not contributing to the running of our nation, or are we going to stop this unfair process?

As the above chart illustrates most profoundly, the upward spiral of negative spending put on the backs of taxpayers already burdened with state income taxes, sales and use taxes of every description, and real estate taxes on their homes, is completely out of control and grossly unfair to the people of the United States.

The gravy train must end, and end soon before the entire nation is strapped into a quagmire; the only escape from which, would be bankruptcy, or worse, revolution and civil war.

> *The first requisite of a good citizen*
> *in this Republic of ours is that he shall*
> *be able and willing to pull his own weight.*
> *—Theodore Roosevelt ,1902*

THE FAMILY

In my young years, my family was the only society I had communication with. Later I added neighborhood and school friends, but still the anchor in my life was my loving parents, sister, aunts, uncles, grandparents, and cousins. We depended on each other for moral and social support.

We celebrated each other's birthdays, anniversaries, religious, and national holidays. These are the fond memories I recall from my childhood. This structure is a far cry from a large segment of today's society.

The schools and churches no longer have the influence they used to have, and our social mores reflect that change.

I am not trying to say that I came from a perfect world. There has always been divorce, cheating, stealing, drunkenness, prostitution, drugs, and other forms of antisocial behavior, but with a solid family unit, my family and I were able to sort out the good from the bad, and the right from the wrong.

In our contemporary society, it is extremely hard for young people to distinguish the differences.

We are raising an entire generation, where many children are raised by one parent, step-parents, grandparents, uncles, aunts, family friends, and even foster parents. These young people are allowed to run in the streets, and their role models come from the ranks of older, street-wise children who have invented their own society, and an entirely different set of rules.

Some of these children may be socially and morally acceptable, but a great many of these kids are misfits, with a whole different language and set of values — the rule of the streets or jungle!

One just looks at the way these young people dress, the music they listen to, the disrespect they show towards school, authority, and their elders, to perceive that something has changed in America, and changed for the worse.

We learned in our child psychology classes in school that youngsters will "try-out" aberrant behavior to test the older generation's reactions. When they are corrected or punished for that behavior, they then learn that they must conform to the standards of society. When children are not reprimanded for their antisocial behavior by someone they respect, then that antisocial behavior becomes the new standard, until they come up with even more new trials.

You can follow the path in the antigovernment music, the truancy and dropout rates in our schools, and finally in our crime statistics. It's as though we have spawned a generation of misfits that we must support with welfare, penal institutions, and loss of life and property. Enough is enough!

It has long been my opinion that all the pent up hate and frustration built up in a life of young people born and raised in an unstructured childhood finally strikes back at society — regardless of the merit of the cause.

In the second day of the Los Angeles riots in 1992, the Reverend Jesse Jackson flew to Los Angeles and was greeted at the airport by a television reporter who began firing questions at him. He blamed the cause of the riots on a society which abandoned young people.

I agree, in part, with Jackson's statement, however I don't agree with his conclusion. These youngsters were abandoned not by society, but by their own fathers and mothers.

I spent over 30 years recruiting athletes for my former university. Many of these young men lived in poor black and Hispanic neighborhoods. The NCAA changed the recruiting rules in the 1980s prohibiting alumni activity in the recruitment of athletes, but for the years before that rule change, the coaches of the various sports would accompany me to the homes of the athletes, where we would meet them and their guardians. We would proceed to take the recruits and families to dinner at a fashionable restaurant and then proceed to extol the virtues of our athletic and educational programs in hopes that the athletes would sign the "letter of intent" to go to our university.

In the cases of over 90% of the hundreds of young men I tried to recruit from these poor neighborhoods (not all athletes elected to choose our school), when it came time to meet the guardian, out came a grandmother or an aunt, or a foster parent. When we inquired about the whereabouts of parents, we were usually told stories of abandonment, or child abuse, or worse. In only about 10% of the cases I witnessed, did I actually meet one or more natural parents.

As an aside to my ventures into these neighborhoods, I would see young children playing or hanging around the streets on school nights, sometimes as late as 11 or midnight after we came back from a lengthy dinner.

I asked the coach I was with, "How can these kids do their homework or other school preparation if they are playing out in the streets all night?" I would usually get a shrug of the shoulders or a blank stare in return.

These youngsters of the 50s, 60s and 70s are now the occupationally dysfunctional adults of today, who constantly argue in the media that society hasn't given them a "break."

The men and women can't read, write, or perform simple arithmetic problems. I was told in my youth that if I didn't get an education, I would be a bum and an outcast from society. Today's young people don't hear the same messages that were told to me, and they wouldn't choose to believe it. Now they want a free lunch.

The problems don't end just with these dysfunctional people. Illegitimacy is at an all time high in the United

States. We can look forward to even greater numbers of misfit children who can't help but grow up hating their parents, their relatives, and society. These youngsters are already committing crimes such as drug dealing, robbery, and even murder. According to Senator Moynihan of New York, a recent study found that 62% of the children in the city of Los Angeles and 79% of the children in Detroit are in families on welfare. Other urban areas have similar statistics.

Nine and ten year-old kids are walking around with guns and knives and killing and wounding each other, as well as other innocent people. The mayhem continues to escalate. When will it end?

Certainly, it won't end with a lot of media diatribe "exposing" the terrible problems besetting our youth. The politicians running for office rarely miss stating the woeful circumstances facing our nation, but once the campaign is over, they go back to "Business as usual," meanwhile the problems facing our youth grow exponentially.

We must have a plan to end the illiteracy, violence, and family breakups or our nation will not survive into the next century.

When parents are not there to supervise their children, a vacuum is thereby created and left to be filled with a street solution. In some cases, children may be fortunate enough to meet older, good kids who provide leadership to help guide these children through their growing years.

Sometimes organizations such as the YMCA or other boy's or girl's clubs set up by civic leaders or school organizations are able to direct youngsters into sports or other activities set up to help them from running in the streets. As a former board member and President of a YMCA, I am quite aware of the large numbers of children left unsupervised by anyone. It is these young people who are in the most danger of following the wrong influence.

It is these bad influences that lead children to come together and form gangs. These gangs become a lawless society unto themselves, and it is my belief that once young people get attached to a gang discipline, the chances of them getting any educational skills are substantially diminished. In fact, once these kids have a couple of brushes with the criminal justice system, they are well under way to being life-long criminals. In a good many cases no combination of education or other societal functions can bring them back to being useful citizens.

This cycle must be broken, and broken soon lest we spawn a whole new generation of gangsters who will be strong enough and well-armed enough to challenge even the United States Army.

We can no longer use platitudes to get out of this dilemma; we must mobilize all the resources of the American people to get behind an effort to teach civil behavior to these youngsters whose language, dress, music, morals, and very existence is taught to them by angry and hateful misfits.

We cannot incarcerate an entire generation. We must have a plan, and then we must execute this plan — and all must participate, not just a few dedicated public servants.

We are all culpable. Therefore we must *all* be prepared to share in the solution; or we will face extinction as a powerful and proud nation.

OUR CHILDREN — OUR TOMORROW?

Many of our problems with our children began with both parents having to work. The burden of taxation, inflation, and erosion of the dollar has made it almost mandatory that women enter the workplace just to help pay the bills.

In Chapter 4, I spoke about how government continues to chug along, taxing, spending, and feeding itself at the cost of its citizens. This is going to have to stop.

1. We must eliminate the Internal Revenue Service, and along with it the income tax as we have known it.

2. We must have sunset laws, on all departments of every level of government: Federal, State, County, City, and Village. Just to keep a department around because it has been in business for a long time is not an answer — it's an excuse. If a government department cannot prove its usefulness, it must be eliminated.

3. We must insist on term limits for all elected officials. If the President of the United States is limited to two — 4 year terms, then so should every other elected official in the nation, with no exceptions. This way an elected official is unable to build his own private dynasty.

4. The Judiciary should be subject to review every four years and those judges who render unwise decisions consistently should be replaced.

These above four points, if executed fairly and correctly, should reduce the cost of running all levels of government, and thus give a great deal of money back to the people. This additional money would allow most women to go back and raise their own children.

We must not wait until a child commits a crime to exercise society's authority upon him. By the time that child has been caught for his or her misdeeds he or she probably already is a hardened criminal.

My solution to this problem is broad-based and very costly — but so is our criminal justice system. I believe in preventing crime before it begins—in early childhood.

Let us follow this proposed program I envision carefully and see how it would work.

When children first enter school in kindergarten or first grade, a competent teacher can usually spot the two or three trouble makers in a class of 30 or 40.

As the semester progresses, if these children are still exhibiting antisocial behavior after being disciplined (as opposed to just being talkative etc.), the teacher should report his or her findings to one of the school administrators.

The administrators should then send these findings to the local social worker's office which, would check to see the specifics regarding the home life of these troublemaking youngsters.

We hear of children who go to school every day without any breakfast. Many of these children are being raised by a poor grandmother, aunt, or some family friend, and often there is no one around who takes particular interest in the child.

If the social worker delivers a report on a child which does not conform with some minimum criteria, then the child's case would be submitted to a court of competent jurisdiction with the ultimate intent to make the child a ward of the state.

Once this program gets going in all 50 states, it is easy to envision hundreds of thousands of kids being made wards of their respective states.

It is this writer's opinion that the foster home program being used in most communities does not work, and the funds being used, for the most part, are not giving the taxpayers value received.

It is my thought that each state should use surplus army bases to build new schools with the principles used in Boys' Town, Nebraska. We could call them Kids' Towns or Youth Schools, but at no time should they have the taint of reform schools or schools for errant kids.

These military bases already have all of the infrastructure in place, and they also have enough permanent buildings and dormitories, so that large expenditures for new school buildings would not be needed.

The most important part of this program would be in the selection of the teachers and the administrators. I would suggest that preference should be given to married teacher couples, who could show, by their leadership, the true values of family living. They would be the family role models the children could observe as they are growing up.

These teachers should be the most experienced men and women we have, and we should pay them the same kind of salary we would pay to our top engineers, who, for years, made implements of war. This program cannot fail —we must have the best, and we must be willing to pay the highest wage. (I would suggest $75,000-$100,000 annually in 1996 dollars to begin, with incremental raises based on performance and inflation.)

The costs of setting up this program will not be cheap, but if we do away with the Federal Department of Education, and other wasteful and very costly unproductive government departments at all levels of government, we will have more than enough money to educate these children, and give them a real chance to enter society with the proper educational tools.

The only alternative I see in continuing with the status quo is to hire more police and build more jails.

I would choose those teachers from a vast ethnic diversity so that mix of cultures is reflected in the school community.

As a former music teacher and professional musician, I have long believed that the reason of the demise of the arts in our youth has been linked with the elimination of music and other fine arts from mostly our large urban area schools. Culture cannot be gained in a vacuum. Art and music, like many of the skills of our American civilization, must be taught. Therefore, it should be part of the curriculum of these schools to bring in the best teachers of art, music, dance and the other arts so that these youthful minds may have exposure to the finer things.

Field trips should be taken to museums, concerts, opera, ballet, theater, etc. to expose the arts to children. Also fine guest artists could be invited to perform and give lectures in their fields of expertise.

The proper balance of all academic subjects, particularly civics (in the higher grades), should be required so that upon graduation from 12th grade, these young people will be prepared to either enter a college, trade school, university, or at least, they would be prepared for living in our American society.

This program may have to run for at least 25 to 50 years in order to weed out those antisocial influences which have plagued our nation for numbers of years. We have tried many other options, and crime and illiteracy is more prevalent today than it ever was.

Yet what is to be done to those young people who are not yet in kindergarten or first grade. We must answer that question on a case by case basis. It would be counterproductive, for instance, to bring in some 10 year olds who have already become exposed to some gang experience, because a few of those children could influence all the rest of the new kids. These decisions would have to be made by the teachers, the social workers, and maybe, even the courts.

The whole point of the program is to separate the innocent young away from an obvious cycle of gangs, crime, incarceration, and a life of criminal activity.

In the absence of parents, schools, churches, or any of the conventional means to civilize our youth, the state must take a compassionate, and expensive, hand in developing a generation or two of worthwhile citizens. By using this model, the educated youth, could join the mainstream of society as useful citizens. They could return to their communities and serve as role models to their children and other children in their neighborhood.

This program would dramatically reverse the negative cycle now in place in most cities.

> *"Human history becomes more and more a race between education and catastrophe."*
> *–H.G. Wells, 1920*

THE DOLLAR TRAP

For most of the 20th Century, the U.S. Dollar was the standard currency value measure for the world. All other currencies were denominated according to "dollar" value. A common figure of speech was describing things being "as sound as a dollar." When is the last time you heard that statement?

When Franklin D. Roosevelt assumed the presidency in 1933, our nation, along with most of the rest of the world, was in a deep financial depression. The bottom had fallen out of the stock market, and former gainfully employed people were out of work, and waiting in bread and soup lines for food handouts to survive starvation.

President Roosevelt was forced to take some emergency measures to keep the nation from falling into even further decline. Among these measures were edicts to close all of the banks and take the country off the gold standard.

He replaced gold as the "coin of the realm" with more plentiful silver. All of the gold was "called in" by the government, and it became a crime to even own gold. The only exceptions were gold coin dealers and collectors of rare coins. Jewelry manufactures and dentists could purchase small quantities of gold to use in their trades, but gold could no longer be legally used to pay bills, groceries or any other commodities.

The price the government set for the repurchase of everyone's gold was $20.00 per ounce. Once all of the gold collected was safely stored in Fort Knox and other holding places, Roosevelt marked up the price of gold to $35.00 per ounce, thereby cheating the American people out of $15.00 per ounce, or 40% of its previous value.

The government then began to print paper money to represent the new silver currency. Problems arose when it was discovered that most coins were alloys, containing little or no silver, and more importantly, the government could turn on the printing presses and print as many greenbacks as they were pleased to print, with no checks and balances to oversee their operations.

This was the beginning of an inflationary spiral which has gained momentum, and today threatens the very financial existence of our nation.

To the average American, inflation of the money supply merely was taken as a necessary step in life. We had to pay more for goods and services, therefore we had to earn more money to pay for these added costs. In the beginning the price and wage increases were insignificant, and most citizens went along with mild inflation because it didn't change their life style significantly.

Our elected officials discovered that they could add bureaus and agencies of government, and staff them with salaried personnel, who were given expense accounts, perks, automobiles, and even airplanes, and the taxpayers didn't object, except for a few minor watchdog groups.

Roosevelt urged the Congress to set up the Work Projects Administration (W.P.A.) whose responsibility it was to create jobs building, and repairing streets and highways, bridges, public buildings and a whole list of public projects. Many thousands of our grateful citizens were taken off of relief roles, and regained their pride by being able to take home a paycheck.

Other projects proposed by Roosevelt such as the National Recovery Act (N.R.A.), were turned down by Congress, but one law he proposed went sailing through Congress and was put into effect in 1935. That law was the Social Security Act.

If you sat down and examined Social Security in the light of day, you would see that it is a Ponzi or pyramid scheme. Any attorney or mathematician could explain that the reason a chain letter, or merchandise pyramid schemes are illegal is that by the time the chain gets down to the base of the pyramid, there aren't enough people on the planet to continue the program.

The same mathematics holds for Social Security. It is impossible to pay off the people at the base of the pyramid: the younger generations.

Another problem with Social Security is the built-in unfairness of the program.

When a person enters the legitimate work force he is mandated (forced) to pay into the Social Security system. He has no other options.

Many millions of people die before reaching their 65th birthday, and if they do not have a surviving spouse, who would be the beneficiaries of the money they had to pay for over 40 years? The answer is nobody.

Their children or grandchildren never get to see a penny of the money, except for a small burial allowance. The rest of the money gets eaten up by the system.

As we have learned recently, the Social Security system is broke. Our good old politicians, in their infinite wisdom, squandered the trust money on their favorite pork barrel projects, and left the American people with a bookkeeping entry, which is supposed to represent the Social Security *Trust Account.*

If someone in the banking, insurance, or real estate industries ever frittered away fiduciary monies entrusted to their keeping, they would be thrown in jail for embezzlement. The government has done just that with impunity. How can we not call people who perform crooked acts crooks?

Now that we have determined that a ponzi or pyramid scheme does not work even if it is run by the government, it is time to go back to the drawing board and fashion a program that is more fair, equitable, and financially sound.

Each individual should establish an insurance program with a private company, therefore his heirs are the beneficiaries of his insurance policy. This program could be overseen by the government the same way pension programs are administered. This way, people who do not live to the age of 65 are not cheated out of their contributions. Those who live longer would have an income equal to, or larger than social security. In any event, the funds would be out of the hands of greedy politicians.

This privatizing social security would work like Individual Retirement Plans (IRA), a program which most workers in America are familiar.

The country of Chile was facing the same financial crises the U. S. is now concerned about. In 1981, the government of Chile was advised by American educated Chilean economists to allow workers to opt out of the government system and invest for retirement in IRAs.

All benefits under Chile's private system are raised annually by a cost-of-living adjustment. This has been possible because the investments in the individual accounts have outpaced inflation.

Seizing on Chile's experience, Argentina and Peru are implementing private systems, and there is support for such reform in the United States as well.

"Chile has demonstrated that a private option for Social Security can be highly successful and beneficial," says Norman Ture, former U. S. Undersecretary of the Treasury.

The Depression ended with the start of World War II when the country went on a war footing.

Defense plants, armaments producers, food and clothing companies were all put into the war effort. Money began to flow down to all strata of society. At one time, 15 million men and women were conscripted into the armed services, and their wages went into the cash flow of the country. Little attention was paid to pork barrel projects or outrageous overcharging of materials, as long as we won the war.

The bureaus and agencies of government which were set up as Depression emergencies or wartime agencies never seemed to be disbanded once the crises were over. The slick government lawyers and bureaucrats merely put a new wrapper on the agencies, asked for more money. Once alive, these agencies never died.

When we went to war in 1941, the government began to sell War Bonds to our patriotic citizens. The most common denomination was the $25.00 bond which sold for $18.75, and paid its face value in 10 years.

Bonds were advertised and sold everywhere. Movie theatres had "buy war bonds and savings stamps" messages right on the screen at the end of each movie. The lights would be turned on in the theater, and bonds and stamps were sold on the spot.

Savings stamps were sold in schools, and each class room would compete against each other room for collection of the most stamps and bonds sold per week, month, and semester.

Workers were asked to volunteer a portion of their pay each week to be set aside for bonds or stamps. The mobilization was complete. Movie and recording stars would make personal appearances and raise millions of dollars selling bonds. It was our "patriotic duty" to contribute towards the war effort.

The $25.00 and other war bonds, when redeemed on their 10th anniversary, had less purchasing power than the original $18.75 investment. The government had played another cruel trick on their own people. Inflation had caused the $25.00 to have less buying power in goods and services than $18.75 had previously purchased.

Ever since Roosevelt devalued the dollar in 1933, the dollar and all instruments denominated in dollars have returned a lessor value in ensuing years than were originally invested.

Besides government bonds, the American public had invested in insurance, stocks, money markets, mutual funds, savings accounts and myriad of other dollar denominated instruments, only to find that the diminished value of the dollar has usually returned less than a fraction of the original investments in real buying power.

Through the tremendous power of media advertising, combined with government platitudes, our gullible citizenry have fallen into what I label The "dollar trap."

We invest into dollar denominated instruments in good faith and hear phrases such as "long term security," "peace of mind," "prudent savings plans," and "conservative planning." All the while, the value of the dollar continues to plummet so that by the time we need to use those investments, we find that inflation and erosion of the dollar have all but destroyed our life's savings. Unfortunately, we can't turn back the clock and make different choices. Betting the dollar will keep its value has caused a good part of the economic strife in this nation, particularly among our elderly.

Americans have always planned for their future retirement years, and there have been many investment vehicles available to them for retirement; things such as insurance, savings accounts in banks, stocks, bonds, mutual funds, and a large mix of what I call dollar-denominated instruments.

Say a 30 year old person in 1955 decided to purchase an insurance annuity which, at age 65, will pay him and his wife $400.00 per month for life.

He calculated that by the time he reached 65, his children would be financially independent and his home would have been paid for.

Based on 1955 prices, $400.00 per month, plus his and his wife's social security, together with some savings, stocks, and bonds, should have taken care of him the rest of his life.

In other words, this typical American family focused their entire program on dollar values and dollar costs for 1955 and beyond. What a tragic error that was!

In 1955, the ordinary first class postage stamp was 3¢; by 1991 it was 29¢, and by this writing it is 32¢. All other prices of goods and services have risen accordingly.

A Chevrolet sedan sold for $1,250.00 in 1955. Today it is closer to $20,000.

A doctor charged $5.00 per office visit and a specialist charged $7.50 to $8.00. Today those same doctors charge from $50.00 to $100.00 per visit.

Inflation applies to all other goods and services. In short, it would take at least $4,000.00 per month for a typical family to just stay even with the market prices, and retain the purchasing power they expected from their $400 per month investment in life insurance.

There is no way our imaginary family can turn back the clock and choose our inflation-sensitive investments, such as real estate or land, they are financially strapped, and the longer they live, the worse off they will be.

In 1955, if the wage-earner of the house earned from $200 to $400 per month, the family could have purchased a home in a nice neighborhood, (not a mansion, of course), owned a car, and lived a comfortable standard of living. The wife could elect whether or not to go to work.

Most of the people caught in the "dollar trap," who are now retired, are in deep poverty. The government destroyed our national wealth through waste and mismanagement, and our very productive middle class has been dealt a blow from which they will never recover, because they are too old to go back to work, or to try other investment options. It was the reliance on dollar denominated investments which has caused this dilemma.

Inflation and Erosion

I have already given some examples of how inflation has destroyed dollar-denominated investment instruments. The most basic definition of inflation is increasing the supply of money.

A less understood phenomena is erosion of the dollar. With inflation we have some options for improvement.

When steak goes to $4.00 per pound, we can purchase chicken or fish. When a new model car sells for $1,000.00 more than the previous model, we can either fix up our old car or purchase a less expensive model. We have choices.

With erosion, there are no options.

In January 1994, the Japanese yen was valued at 135 yen to the dollar. Seven months later the yen was only 95 to the dollar.

It is as though a bandit came in the middle of the night and robbed us of approximately 40% of our dollar value, and we had absolutely no say in the matter.

Meanwhile, our representatives in Washington continued business as usual.

As we discussed in previous chapters, politicians are only concerned about being re-elected, and they will use any means at their disposal to hoodwink our people into thinking that everything is all right.

Well, everything is not all right!

They keep spending tax payers' money at an alarming rate, and our trade deficits continue to remain well over $100 billion per year with no relief in sight.

Other smaller nations, such as Taiwan, have a positive balance of payments, and they don't have to tax their citizens into poverty. People in such nations as Taiwan, Japan, Germany, Singapore, and many other countries have encouraged their citizens to save and invest for the future. These nations are prospering, while we have become a bankrupt welfare state with a negative balance of payments.

This destruction of the dollar both from within our nation and globally, has caused part of the dilemma we now face.

When wives and mothers were literally forced into the workplace in the late 1960s, the entire social structure of the family changed. After working a full day, the mother and father had little time or patience to spend with their children.

This was about the time we began to see youth gangs, crime, and drugs escalate exponentially. Without parents available to supervise their children, we have seen the breakdown of American family, and hence, of our society.

The government's destruction of the value of our money supply can be seen as the direct cause of the breakdown of the American family. The tensions within the family structure, because both parents in the work force, is a mitigating cause of much of our divorce rate, and this will continue to increase until one income can again support the family.

Before I get thousands of letters from angry career women, let me qualify my statements. Those women who prefer to pursue careers should certainly continue to do so. I am speaking, however, about those many women who are *forced,* by family economics, to go into the work force. These are the women who would prefer to stay home and raise their kids. They should not have to work if they don't wish to.

We are witnessing the usual hypocrisy of the government when our elected leaders point fingers at our families and blame them for the breakdown of our society. It has been the government's own mismanagement and waste of our hard earned money that has caused this strain on the American family.

The waste and pork barrel projects that have developed over the past 50 years are the repugnant legacy left by selfish, arrogant and self-serving government officials. This vast amount of wealth squandered in the name of "the public good" must serve as a warning to all taxpayers that when left to their own devices, our elected and nonelected officials merely invent reasons to spend our hard earned money, and as long as we don't protest, they continually ask for more.

In the 1960s a man by the name of Ralph Nader began to criticize the safety of some American-made automobiles. He testified before Congressional Committees, very often on television and through his lambasting of the automobile industry, he invented the "consumer protection" movement.

What he and Congress failed to mention in those early days of "consumerism" is that the regulations, rules, and laws thereby instigated, caused the prices of everything, regulated, to go up.

Because of the retooling, paperwork and other higher costs, these costs were passed on to the consumer. They never disclosed to the consumers that when all those rules were passed — options such as, would you like to pay $2,000, $3,000, $4,000 or more for a consumer protected auto, or would you like to save that money?

Most of the situations that Nader and his people were using were based on two or three accidents in 100,000 autos. The drama portrayed, by those accidents caused our representatives to over react to the real need of those laws.

A side issue which resulted from those laws was the fact that our would-be competitors, such as Japan and Germany, had no such laws, and therefore, they could put out products more cheaply then the American companies, thus putting American jobs, American families supported by those jobs, and the American economy at a disadvantage.

Mr. Nader invented a new term in the English language. He told Congress, the media, and anyone else who would listen, that American business was "ripping-off" the public.

This became the catch phrase of the 1960s, 1970s and 1980s. The outcome of that phrase had far reaching results well beyond the imagination of Mr. Nader. We have thus far lost hundreds upon thousands of businesses to overseas countries, thereby costing our people millions of jobs.

Nobody apparently explained to our Congress that when you increase regulations and rules to the likes of General Motors or Ford, they merely raise the prices and pass on the added costs to the consumers. But when you lay heavy rules and restrictions on small and medium sized businesses, such as existed in the clothing, shoes, and other labor intensified industries, they either go out of business, or remove themselves to offshore manufacturing facilities.

In either case, the American jobs market, families, consumers, and the economy are the losers. These companies are gone, and they will never return.

Large retail department stores and furniture chains went out of business. When people are out of work, who is left to shop for finished goods?

This reprehensible term of "rip-off" is also responsible for pitting consumers against business of all kinds. In another words, we have another case of government pitting one group against another.

In the early 1970s we were told by our officials in Washington that we had an oil crisis. The consequences of this "crisis" caused long lines at gasoline stations and various forms of gas rationing occurred. The country was facing a lack of oil supplies, and a full blown recession came about as the by-product of that crisis.

The truth of the matter was, that while the President, Congress, and Department of Energy were bemoaning the crisis in the media, long lines of oil tankers were kept offshore, restrained from off-loading their cargo. There was never an oil shortage — just a bunch of Washington bureaucrats trying a power play against the oil producing nations (OPEC), and once the price of oil was raised, the "crisis" ended.

In the meantime, hundreds of thousands of jobs were lost, and many industries and smaller businesses were forced to curtail or shut down their activities.

All of this was caused by our elected officials and their appointed stooges. They invented an oil crisis, and when the oil producers didn't fall for their bluff, the crisis ended, but at the cost of much suffering.

Who appointed those people to manage the destiny of the marketplace, or the free enterprise system? There is nothing in the Constitution which entitles these people to macro-manage our economy and then throw it into recession. Whenever government has gotten into the business world, prices have gone up and efficiency has fallen way down. The most efficient branch of government, according to Washington, is the Postal Department, and it only operates at 80% efficiency. It sometimes takes longer to get a letter from the other side of town than to the other side of the country.

When President Reagan assumed office in 1981, he inherited the recession of the 1970s. In order to jump-start the economy, he came out with a whole list of ideas, one of which was to allow commercial real estate a 15 year depreciation schedule instead of the previous 30 years depreciation.

This great tax incentive took the nation right out of the recession. Commercial and residential development and investment ran at an all time high, and the nation was blessed with its greatest prosperity in history.

Some greedy developers and savings and loans found ways to take unfair advantage of this new tax loophole, and began to build commercial real estate just for the sake of building, with no regard for the need or merit of the projects.

Congress, instead of restraining the errant perpetrators, decided to not only repeal the 1981 act, they completely reversed their previous incentives of owning real estate, and then caused a series of disincentives.

The previous tax incentives of using depreciation (both accelerated for 15 years and life of the building, usually 30 years) were repealed. This caused most commercial real estate investments such office buildings, shopping centers, apartment houses and even homes purchased as investments and leased out to families to drop in value. It has been traditional in the real estate business to use the tax incentives as part of the motivation to own commercial real estate. Without these incentives, commercial real estate is less valuable.

This is a favorite Washington ploy, when the use of a fly swatter will do the job, Congress and the bureaucrats use a cannonade.

When Congress "changed its mind" in 1986 and passed laws to *disallow* tax deductions for all commercial real estate, they also passed the *word* on to the banks, savings and loans and insurance companies who held the financing on those properties not to renew the loans.

For example, if a bank or insurance company would finance an office building, for seven or ten years, after which time the loan would be "called," this usually meant that a new loan would be negotiated. This new loan would sometimes be at a higher interest rate or the bank would charge "loan points" as a fee for rolling over the loan for another seven or ten years.

This has been commonplace in the commercial loan field for years. This is unlike an owner occupied home mortgage, which usually has a 20 to 30 year fixed loan. The banks rarely "call" a residential loan before the property is paid off, unless the property is resold, and the new owner must get new financing.

When the government decided to throw a monkey wrench into the commercial real estate business, they advised their member banks and insurance companies not to roll over these loans as they came due.

The owners of the properties either had to pay off the existing loans or face the loss of their properties. In the late 80s and early 90s, nearly a trillion dollars' worth of commercial real estate was lost by investors, most of whom had never missed an installment payment, or had defaulted on their loans.

It is interesting to note that because of Mr. Reagan's 1982 tax law, vast sums of money were taken out of the stock market, mutual funds and insurance portfolios, and reinvested in the very lucrative real estate market.

The 1986 double-cross was orchestrated by the various Congressional members who were in the back pocket of the very powerful stock market and insurance lobbyists. The fact that millions of people lost their life's savings, or that savings and loans and banks went bankrupt, or that the tax payers were faced with a trillion dollar loss, meant nothing to these insensitive money-hungry people.

The consequences of their actions bankrupted thousand of savings and loans, banks, real estate developers and brought on the recession of the 1990s, the consequences of which are still being felt, all because of a ruthless and insensitive Congress.

Then the Congress invented the RTC, Resolution Trust Corporation, a government agency which virtually trashed much of the savings and loan and real estate developments.

Office buildings, apartment houses, homes, land, and many businesses were sold off by the RTC for a fraction of their actual worth, thus costing not only the investors in these enterprises their life savings, but also destroying the commercial real estate market.

When the Government tries to get into the business of business, everyone loses.

The fault lies, for the most part, on the selfishness and greed of politicians and the bureaus and agencies of government.

Unless our country is able to return to a solid financial economy and return the dollar to a place of respect in the world, our economy is going to collapse like a house of cards, and no power on earth will be able to save future generations.

Back in the years after World War I, much of the philosophy in America favored isolationism. In a world economy, which is also an information-relating community, isolationism is equivalent to a nations' suicide.

We must be prepared to compete at all levels. Therefore, our first resolve must be to have a positive balance of payments.

Secondly, we must bring the dollar back to its former prominence.

Finally, we must significantly reduce the national debt.

All of these goals could be accomplished if we reduce the size of government at all levels. We could eliminate thousands of agencies and eliminate hundreds of thousands of jobs, which do little or nothing to improve our society.

Agencies at the federal level such as The Department of Education, the Department of Highways, the Department of Housing and Urban Development and countless other bureaus and agencies at State, County and City levels are weakening our national wealth.

It is very difficult to have ambition and incentive to get ahead when you realize that your hard-earned rewards are being squandered by an insensitive government and bureaucrats. This is particularly reprehensible, when we see the idlers and nonproductive of our citizens (and illegals), reaping the rewards that were earned by the hard-working, and productive tax payers.

We must eliminate the income tax as soon as possible and replace it with a point-of-sale tax. As previously stated, this type of tax forces everyone to pay a share of running the government.

We must also return to a method of stabilizing the dollar. The present method of having paper money guarantee other paper money is a sham, and must be corrected if our people are ever going to get a fair and legitimate shake for their money. I would suggest our government going back either to a gold or silver standard so that our present fiat money is backed by something solid, otherwise we will continue to allow our wealth to be plundered and our people impoverished.

If we are going to re-civilize America, we are going to have to begin by eliminating the incongruities of our burgeoning welfare state and take the government once and for all out of the marketplace. As illustrated in this chapter, every time the government gets involved in the marketplace, the American people suffer.

> *"A billion here, a billion there, and pretty soon*
> *you are talking about real money."*
> *–Sen. Everett M. Dirksen (1896-1969)*

HATE

A house divided against itself cannot stand.
—Abraham Lincoln

During the first half of the 20th Century, our nation fought in two World Wars, and during and immediately after each of these wars, we were united as a people like we never have been. A very distinct American nationality emerged after our international engagements, and it appeared that we had finally eliminated the yoke of petty hatred which plagued our nation's earlier years.

Each time a new ethnic group arrived upon our shores, they had to fight their way through intolerance, bigotry, and hate until they finally earned a modicum of acceptance into the "American society."

First the Irish, then the Germans, Eastern Europeans, the Jews; the blacks; the Hispanics; and finally the

Asians. Each new group had to find housing, jobs, schooling for their children, and business and professional enterprises for themselves.

This usually involved a two — generation assimilation period until the second generation matriculated through American schools and were able to dress, speak, and carry on in the idioms of the majority. The poking fun (and worse) at foreign accents and different customs seemed to melt into the past as new generations of "Americans" were able to take their places alongside the rest of the people.

Minor hate and jealousy incidents occurred along the way, but the rank and file of the most of our countrymen showed patience and tolerance.

Even the wounds of the Civil War seemed to ameliorate themselves during and after World War II.

Great black figures such as world heavyweight champion, Joe Louis; United Nations representative, Ralph Bunche; baseball player, Jackie Robinson; Civil Rights Champion, Dr. Martin Luther King Jr., and many other prominent educators and professionals seemed to dominate the high ground for the last great conflict to finally eliminate the hatred and bigotry against a group of people whose only difference was that they were born with a different color of skin.

What started out as a war against hate, however, has escalated to a myriad of new hate groups, each armed with its own agenda, and bent upon getting its own way.

1. We have women versus men groups.
2. Old versus young groups.
3. Black versus white groups.

4. White versus black groups.
5. "Americans" versus foreign groups.
6. Armed militants versus the government groups.
7. Urban gangs versus other urban gangs fighting for turf.
8. Discrimination versus reverse discrimination.
9. Consumer groups versus business.
10. Union groups versus employers.

And the list goes on and on.

When you look at this limited list, you can easily find yourself in a group which is under some sort of pressure or stress. We no longer are a nation of a large majority and a few minorities.

EVERYONE IS A MINORITY!

Between government and the media, every small incident which illustrates intolerance, hate, and bigotry, seems to be illuminated and enlarged upon. A group is expected to voice its opinions in dramatic fashion for the mass media.

We have all seen protest marches, union demonstrations, or other radical outbursts which only last long enough for the media to photograph, televise, or interview some of the leaders, and then suddenly these "staged" events break up as soon as the media leaves.

Once the message has gone out to the masses, the job has been done. It is not my intention to belittle or deny anyone's right to free speech or assembly, but merely to point out that without mass media aiding and abetting these divergent pressure groups, a more civilized approach could be used to address their grievances.

Movies and television stories are contrived to further splinter our society into camps. Violence, drugs, crime, rapes, bombings, insurrections, and all of the entire range of aberrant behavior is shown, particularly to our very impressionable young people, many of whom go right out and "try out" this sort of behavior for themselves.

If we are going to re-civilize our nation, we are going to have to reduce the passion of our zeal to within more reserved bounds. One does not have to bomb a church or school in order to get one's message across.

Moreover, the responsible leaders of government and the media must develop a high level of standards which could serve as a framework through which civilized dialogue can be exchanged. Tabloid journalism has only aided in tearing down our social structure.

A standard of restraint must be adopted to show our young people an example of civilized comportment . It is very difficult to teach young people a restrained and civilized way to conduct themselves if they only witness their elders behaving like barbarians.

In the last half of the 20th century, two new major hate groups have become a part of our society. Children from broken homes and the homeless and dysfunctional illiterates. Each one of these groups has, and continue to have, an even greater negative effect on our American Civilization. I would like to discuss each of these groups briefly.

Broken Homes: There was a time when divorce was frowned upon by society. Most people were aware that the major casualties from a divorce were the children.

Instead of insisting on family units remaining intact, divorce laws have been materially relaxed so as to allow people to divorce as easily as discarding an old pair of shoes.

As I discussed earlier, the government policies which almost require both partners in a marriage to bring home a paycheck, have been one of the major causes of family breakups. In the years when only one salary was sufficient to support the family, divorce was substantially less frequent than in later years, when the women were forced into the labor pool.

It is not easy to keep track of the activities of young, school-aged children when both parents are out working all day. These children can and do get into all sorts of mischief in the streets. Drugs, gangs, and criminal behavior are only some of the problems which occur.

We have invented terms such as "latchkey children" to describe these lonely kids who must come home from school, admit themselves into a home, and remain alone until one or more of the parents returns. It isn't long until some of these children figure out some "creative" things to do. The terrible psychological impact that is thrust upon young immature minds begins to give rise to some of the terrible antisocial behavior we have witnessed the last 20 to 30 years.

Ten and 11 year-old kids drink alcohol, use drugs, shoot guns at other kids, and so forth. Crime among children has become a ghastly uncomplimentary statistic in our nation, and the numbers are on the rise. The children of those children grow up to be even worse statistics.

The unknowing parent is legend. When these people are summoned to the police stations to face their errant children, one can witness genuine astonishment. They thought that they were a "good family," hard-working, and raising "good kids." By now, their awareness is usually too late.

We have many children in our nation who are hardened criminals before they reach their teens.

A very large number of our homeless and dysfunctionally illiterate people are those very same children who are from broken homes or who did not get the benefit of their education because they found it easier to run the streets in their youth. These are the dropouts of society who have invented a sub-society dependent upon pan handling, government handouts and crime.

A small minority of these people used to be in mental institutions, but their sheer weight in numbers can no longer be accommodated by the limited number of state supported mental institutions, so they have been set free to wander the streets.

We now have hate groups based on color, ethnicity, age, and sex, and all we do is sit around and talk about it and point fingers.

This is part of the mobilization that I spoke of earlier. We have caused these problems, and now it is up to us to solve them. In a later chapter I plan to list a whole group of solutions. These will not be easy, but if we are to survive as a nation, we must do so.

There is no room in this country for hyphenated Americanism. The one absolutely certain way of bringing this nation to ruin, of preventing all possibility of its continuing to be a nation at all, would be to permit it to become a tangle of squabbling nationalities.
—Theodore Roosevelt, October, 1915

CRIME AND PUNISHMENT

The Second Amendment to the Constitution of the United States, which is part of the first 10 amendments known as the Bill of Rights states:

"A right to keep and bear arms a well regulated militia, being necessary to the security of a free State, the right of the people to keep and bear arms, shall not be infringed."

These amendments were put into law on December 15, 1791. The population of the United States in 1790, according to the first official census of the new nation, was 3,929,000 people, spread very sparsely along the eastern section of the country.

As most of us have learned in our history books, viewed in the movies, and through television portrayals, (both real and fictional) the settling of the rest of the vast country which we now know as the lower 48 states, took over 100 years. The original pioneers who ventured from one area to the next in the Western and Southern movements were constantly beset by warring Indians, dangerous animals, and people from other nations, who also tried to lay claim to their land. We, as a nation, felt that it was our "Manifest Destiny" to control all of the land from the Atlantic to the Pacific, and we had to fight for every mile of the land.

In that untamed wilderness, where sometimes just a few families were pitted against formidable odds, firearms were as necessary as horses or farming implements. The army wasn't able to protect every settlement and stray farm, so it was very important that these people were able to defend themselves.

Never before in the history of the world had such a large land mass been settled and populated in so short a time. Many thousands of settlers and Indians were killed during this western movement, not to mention the thousands who were involved in Mexican Wars in Texas, or the British wars in the Northwest Territory and Canada.

The so-called "militia" usually consisted of the local settlers banding together to defend their communities.

It has been nearly a century since the "West Was Won." We no longer concern ourselves with Indian attacks, and we hire professional police departments and armed services to protect us from criminals and foreign enemies, so what reason do we still have to bear arms?

What we do now is kill each other, and killing each other has become a commonplace state in the past 30 years of the 20th century. Children of elementary school ages are toting guns to school, and shooting at anyone who doesn't please them.

Who hasn't witnessed television news broadcasts of families and loved ones mourning over the death of an innocent child or adult who was killed by vicious teen-agers wielding guns? The father of Michael Jordan, one of the most famous basketball players of our era, was gunned down at an automobile rest area by a couple of punks who decided that "they had to kill someone."

One cannot open a newspaper or listen to a radio or television news broadcast without hearing about random drive-by shootings, showdowns on the street or in bars, or just ordinary people shooting relatives or friends, either by accident, or on purpose.

Guns have become a national scandal, and regardless of the dialogue to the contrary, many thousands of our citizens are killed or maimed everyday. This massacre must stop. All the arguments that blame the "people who shoot the guns" or "the guns don't shoot by themselves.", will not bring those murdered people back to life. You never hear of a drive-by knifing. Cowards can shoot a gun from a distance, and then run away.

It is not important to set down all the bloody statistics; you can read them daily in the newspapers. What is important, is that the families and loved ones of the tens of thousands of needlessly slain people can take little solace in the fact that it is "Constitutionally" all right to own guns.

The Constitution didn't regulate air travel or auto emissions or thousand of other inventions that came about after 1791; so we as a society had to promulgate rules and regulations to apply to those inventions.

By the same reasoning, now that the need to bear arms against the adversities encountered in the expansion of our country from coast to coast, and from Canada to Mexico, has long since been completed, the second Amendment to the Bill of Rights should be reinterpreted forthwith, and all guns, except those used for hunting purposes, should be turned in to the local police and sheriffs. (A simple act of the courts could give wiser meaning to the second Amendment which could avoid changing the Constitution.)

The hunting guns could be kept at various lodges, and monitored by licensed hunters, so that once the hunting season is over, the guns are kept under lock and key in the various lodges.

The gun-related crimes have proven to all who have witnessed the crime, killings, and maiming of the last 30 years, that guns have no place in civilized society.

There are paramilitary groups training in various parts of our nation with the express intent of sparking warfare against the legally elected government of the United States, or against certain cities or states.

The bloodshed in Waco, Texas at the Branch Davidian Compound is just one small example of what can happen when guns are put in the hands of a sect of crazy people, willing to fight to the death of themselves, and everyone around them.

The bombing of the Federal Building in Oklahoma City is another example of our society going haywire.

We have anarchists armed with very sophisticated weaponry ready to do battle against the people of the United States, and they are protected by the "right to bear arms."

If we are going to have a civilized America, we are going to have to begin acting civilly towards each other. We have millions of guns and other armaments out there in the hands of some very irresponsible people, and we must resolve to get rid of those guns, once and for all. Failure to take back our streets and neighborhoods will put our nation into a jungle mentality for many years to come.

My suggest for solutions would be to:

1. Reinterpret the second Amendment to the Bill of Rights through new laws.
2. Pass a national law requiring all guns to be turned into local law enforcement or national guard facilities by a certain date (the same way Franklin Roosevelt required all of the gold to be sold to the banks). The guns could have a dollar value to be determined by the army or law enforcement officials.
3. Failure to turn in all guns by that date would be a felony, and punishable by prison time.
4. If gang activities continue, and drive-by shootings or other crimes occur where guns are used, the governors of each state could declare martial law in those heavy crime districts and order the national guard to sweep complete neighborhoods with door to door searches.

According to Princeton University Professor John J. Dilulio, Jr., the director of the Brookings Institution for

Public Management, an authority on criminal justice, and a widely-read author on crime

1. Up to a third of those convicted of murder across the country were on parole, probation, or some other release at the time they took another person's life.
2. Crime in general is getting more violent. Over the past three decades, your chances of becoming a crime victim have increased 280%. And your chances of becoming a victim of violent crime has increased 460%.
3. The crime problem is bad enough in large cities, but demographic evidence indicates that it is going to get much worse through the country.

Once the gangsters see that our people mean business and we are intent on taking back the streets, school yards, parks, public places, they will either comply with the law, or be forced into prison.

We have coddled those wayward people long enough. It is time to get tough.

I remember when people could stroll in the park or take walks along any street in the United States and feel safe. Today, there are few places left that one can feel safe.

It is time to take back our cities and towns from the lowlifes we have permitted to intimidate us, and the first requirement is getting rid of the guns.

Punishment

The entire criminal justice system has to be streamlined and brought into the 21st century.

The circuses that prevailed in the Rodney King and O. J. Simpson cases are but small microcosms of what is wrong with our system. The old laws regarding juries of our peers has been downgraded to a racial quota system.

I heard comments about the O. J. Simpson case on black talk shows to the effect that "The Brother is not going to be found guilty." Right or wrong — guilt or innocence is no longer the order of the day.

Potential jurists are usually selected from a group of people who do not want to serve on a jury, and we usually wind up with a group of misfits who barely understand what is going on.

It is finally time to get rid of the jury system entirely and substitute a panel of three judges to hear all criminal cases. We have an overabundance of lawyers in the country who would be happy to be paid for their professional services to serve alongside judges.

This way, when a point of law is brought up in court, the long and tedious explanation to a bunch of lay people needn't be exercised. A great deal of time could be saved both in having knowledgeable people sitting in judgment, plus we could avoid having the whole hoopla that occurs when a juror is thrown off the jury and goes public with a lot of useless prattle.

The whole "strategy" of impaneling a jury could be eliminated, thus saving all kinds of time and money. The routine of notifying people by mail that they must serve on a jury, the phone calls and conversations between court and staff and prospective jurors, the costs of going to court and waiting (sometimes weeks) to get on a jury, is a tremendous waste of millions of man/women hours yearly, and, what finally becomes the jury, leaves a lot to be desired.

Our system of selecting juries is about as dumb as impaneling a group of "one's peers" to "vote" on whether the doctor should operate or not. If the jury says yes, then you operate. If the jury votes no, then there won't be an operation.

We live in an age of specialization. Let legally trained people decide the fate of court actions — not a bunch of folks off the streets.

Justice is much too slow, not only during lengthy trials, but also with long-appeals. People who committed murder in the 1980s, are still on death row 10 to 15 years later awaiting legal maneuvering to "protect their rights."

What kind of rights did their victims have? Their sentences were performed in an instant, and the guilty swagger around for years, protected by "rights."

When our youngsters witness all of this, how can we teach them right from wrong? The bad guy gets all of the publicity on television and in the rest of the media. It is at a point where some of these vicious murderers are regarded as folk heroes.

For instance can you name the victims of Geoffrey Daumer or some of the other serial killers?

We are going to have to change our emphasis on good versus evil. The bad guys should be sent straight to their punishment without the media blitzes that occur, and they should be made an example to society that they are the worst of us, not the most famous.

What do we do with hardened criminals, repeat criminals, lifers, and the whole list of antisocial types? It is my opinion that we have a hidden labor force whom the taxpayers have to support with free lodging, food, clothing, recreation, and whole teams of lecturers, psychologists, doctors, nurses, teachers, and other support people.

We have all noted the disrepair and obsolescence of our streets, freeways, highways, bridges, flood control channels, rivers, streams, local and national parks, schools, and colleges (and the list goes on).

With the idle labor pool sitting around at taxpayers' expense, we should be wise enough to figure out an accommodation between the labor unions, and private industry, to put these people to work repairing and rebuilding our nation's infrastructure.

Idle brains can only think of crime and mischief; but when accomplishing useful tasks, a good many of these criminals could earn their way back into society, and also learn the skills of useful trades on their way back. Most of these criminals are school dropouts who never learned the educational basics. Instead of them pumping iron, we should begin to educate these people. We can work out some kind of a point system for the least hardened of the criminals which could go towards their release.

Allowing the criminal justice system to continue on its present course only leads to further astronomical costs which grow geometrically as more and more youths from broken and disadvantaged homes join gangs, commit crimes, and are incarcerated. There is no end to the cycle. The burden on society continues to mount.

The old bleeding-heart methods of trying to rehabilitate criminals by talking to them and showing them right from wrong, has proven to be a failure. What has been missing has been a means which can be used to turn criminals into working citizens.

Like all programs, we cannot be assured of 100% success, but we do know that if given a chance to enter society after having proven skills in the construction and labor field, most of the people who would otherwise turn to crime would become useful members of society.

A civilized society needs to use the resources of all of its citizens, otherwise it is only partially civilized.

EDUCATION

If a nation expects to be ignorant and free,
in a state of civilization, it expects what
never was and never will be.
—Thomas Jefferson

As a former school teacher and the son of a music teacher (who taught for 45 years in the Chicago Public Schools), I can tell you first hand why I left the teaching profession; there was not enough money for the efforts expended. I saw my late father spend a whole career caring about young people and going that extra mile when a youngster needed help, and for the reward of satisfaction.

How can a person be satisfied if he cannot even afford to take a vacation, purchase a new automobile, or retire financially secure with dignity?

I began teaching school in 1951, at the amazing stipend of $3,450.00 per year. That was $66.35 per week before taxes. One day during a recess break I watched some construction workers break up the asphalt street in front of the school, preparatory to repaving. I went up to one of the workers who was stripped to the waist who had stopped working to take a drink of water.

We began chatting and I asked him what kind of wages his kind of work paid. He told me that he made $100.00 per week (or almost 44% more than I made with my Master's degree). I didn't want to inquire as to his educational background, but I was certain that it didn't include any sort of college degree.

My reflections on that incident are still with me more than 40 years later. A society which entrusts their children to a person who makes less money than a person who hammers up the streets must not be too concerned about its children's education.

The people who drive the school buses are paid more than the teachers. So are the garbage collectors.

When our teachers make less money than laborers, what kind of educational standard can our society demand? We hear of the lack of funds to pay teachers; meanwhile we pay a journeyman relief baseball pitcher $1 million or more per year. The lottery jackpot always seems to have tens of millions of dollars from citizens. The gambling Meccas of Las Vegas an Atlantic City, are always teeming with high rollers; the race tracks gambling on horses take in billions every year and people spend fortunes on lavish vacations; but we don't seem to ever have enough money to pay our teachers a decent wage.

My resignation from teaching was a protest against the unfairness of the pay scale, and lack of the advancement in the field. In other words, one started out as a peasant at the low end of society, and after a whole career he was still at the bottom. It was, *Good-bye Mr. Chips,* American style.

A doctor makes more money for a three hour operation than most school teachers earn in a month. The doctor is a professional; what is the teacher? A baby sitter?

If our nation is going to compete in the new global information age, we will have to rethink our priorities. If the pay scale of teacher's wages rivaled that of engineers, doctors, dentists, and athletes we could bring in the most competent people in our nation to teach our children.

Great teachers can motivate our young people to learn and become the best that their abilities will allow. What we have now are kids just sliding by with the least amount of effort and dropping out as soon as it is legally possible. It seems that our whole education system emphasizes mediocrity. When you have mediocre teachers and administrators, what is to be expected of the student?

Only lip service is given to excellence, otherwise it might present a bad example to the rest of the kids and their parents. When I went to school, the kids with outstanding grades or abilities in art or music were showcased in the community. I have seen examples recently when outstanding performance is put down for trying to "show up" their peers.

I would like to begin by saying that although we generally speak of education in the singular, such as my children are getting a high school or college education, it really should be regarded in the complexity of a plural because education is a multifaceted set of experiences.

To many young people, some of the most important social skills they learn are outside of the classroom interacting with their fellow students. Others begin their life careers early in their school years through developing language, mathematics, art or musical skills.

Even though I left the teaching field, I regard education as the most important mission of our society, and it is only through a firm national commitment to education will we be able turn our nation around to again be the envy of the world.

I therefore have broken down this chapter into a series of educational requirements which should be adopted by every board of education in our country as minimum standards. If we are to survive as a cultured civilization, we will only be able to do so through education.

According to many pediatricians and countless educational experts, a child's education may begin while it is still in the womb. Loud noises or good music may do things to the nervous system of the fetus.

But for the sake of this discourse, we will state the traditional opinion that a child's education begins at birth. Everything a child sees in his formative years becomes part of his education.

If the child's parents smoke, drink, attend church regularly, or have a peaceful or tumultuous relationship, these habits becomes part of a child's education.

Unfortunately, most of what we have learned about parental and child relationships are what we have observed in our own families. It is therefore predictable that if a child comes from a family where strong educational and moral values are practiced, it generally will be reflected in the way a child accepts his education.

On the other hand, if all a child observes is abuse, lack of interest in education, use of liquor and/or drugs and a complete lack of moral values, the child of such a family will probably be an educational dropout long before he actually quits school. His course is charted at a very early age. To a great extent we are all products of our environment.

It has long been the philosophy of scholars and theologians that a child's lifelong attitudes are formed by the time he or she reaches their seventh birthday.

In recent years, the dialogue between family, church, and educational leaders has been going on with each faction pointing the finger of responsibility at the other regarding the poor academic showing of our youth. The real answer, in my opinion, is that *all* of society must share the responsibility for what has happened to our children, and we must all share in the solution.

As parents we just cannot send a child in the next room to watch television, or tell him to go out and play, and then expect him to turn into a worthwhile citizen.

It would be the same thing if we wanted to make some furniture, bought the wood and tools then told tell these items to get busy and become furniture.

Raising children is a *full time* occupation and it should be considered, to paraphrase the old General Electric ads, *"our most important product."*

I discussed earlier the disparaging role the government has played in destroying our wealth as a nation, thus forcing both parents into the workplace. This is not something which can be undone by following this book or any series of books.

We are currently in this dilemma, and we must figure out goals to work within these restrictions to save our children.

No fair reading of plummeting test scores, increases of juvenile crime, illegitimate births to teenagers, murder, rape, car-jackings, drive-by shootings, gangs of boys and girls running drugs, and all the other sad statistics can tell us that we are doing a proper job educating and civilizing our youth. In a recent report, U.S. students math test scores ranked 14th against other industrial nations. (I didn't know that there were 13 other industrial nations.) I can remember when we were near the top in all subjects.

The 1994 National Assessment of Educational Progress showed that high school seniors scored "significantly lower" on reading proficiency tests than they did in 1992. The nation's top school official, Secretary of Education Richard Rialey said that the Scholastic Aptitude Tests (SAT) were 46 points lower than they were in 1969, when the slow decline of U. S. Education quality was already well under way.

In 1982, President Reagan's education secretary, Terrell Bell, issued his landmark report A Nation at Risk, declaring that educational decline was a threat to American living standards.

The decline in what young people learn has occurred just at a time when the need to know and perform has never been greater, owing to global economic competition and the introduction of ever higher levels of technology.

The high degree of respect, manners, and consideration that we used to pride ourselves in is completely lacking in the younger generation, and it is getting worse. Things like the etiquette of driving an auto does not even exist in the minds of many teenagers. This is one of the causes of so many auto accidents involving young people. They show absolutely no courtesy to anyone.

These are all things which are taught by others. If children see their parents showing consideration and courtesy to others, then they are likely to emulate that behavior.

We don't think that the children are watching when the adults closest to them display antisocial behavior such as getting drunk, high on drugs, or committing spousal abuse, but don't let us fool ourselves: as the old saying goes, "little pitchers have big ears." And you can add eyes and nervous systems to that as well.

You cannot use vulgar language at home and not expect your kids to use those same words on the street and in school. Children are a mirror of what they see and hear, whether it is at home, school, church, scouts, or the YMCA. Therefore is important that we make it a national commitment to comport ourselves in the best possible fashion so that our children start off on the right foot with an enthusiasm for learning and a positive outlook on life. We must teach our children that they are responsible for their own actions. There is no alibi for failure, if a person is taught initiative and self responsibility

Media and Education

When I was a youngster, the only media we were subject to was radio, newspapers, magazines and some comic books. We would go to the movies with our parents, or to the Saturday matinee with our friends, but all of the entertainment we would see was of the wholesome family variety, with an occasional western shoot-out. However, in all cases the good guys vanquished the bad guys.

Today's generation is subjected to many hours of television per week, most of which portrays mindless violence, perverted morals, and in many cases, portrays the world in an aberrant and distorted fashion. Needless to say, this media exposure is a very important part of our children's education, and much of it comes along before they even enter a classroom.

In the early years of the movies, we had the Hays Board which, in effect, censored what could be said or portrayed on the screen. The whole purpose of The Hays Act was to prevent our children from being bombarded with the sex and violence which we now see on the screen.

It is my opinion that censorship in a free society is not necessary; however, mindful and conscionable adults who make, produce, and finance our movies and television should band together and develop their own standards of what should be aired to our young and impressionable youth. A good place to start is to ask themselves, "Would I want my children and my grand-children to view these programs?"

In these formative years, positive programs such as *Sesame Street,* have done wonders in teaching young people to listen, read, write, learn social studies, music, art, and a number of educational skills before they begin their formal schooling.

The media can serve as a powerful tool for education and the leaders of the industry should be in the forefront of educating our young people. Other nations striving to get a piece of the economic pie, such as Japan, are using tools of the media to help educate their children to be the best students they can be.

American television, movie, newspaper, and radio industries should do no less. In fact, we should be world leaders in advancing educational and moral principles through our media.

When I was taking my courses in education and teacher training at university, there was a running dialogue going on between educators and each had volumes of statistics to back each position. The argument simply stated was; "Should education prepare students for advanced education or should education prepare students for life?"

I always thought that this was a stupid argument. The proponents of the first position stated that those students who graduated high school, went on to university, and then took advanced degrees should only be prepared for that education.

The proponents of the second position stated that students should always be able to fit within their society.

John Dewey, the great pioneer in education said, *"Education is not preparation for life, education is life itself."*

These and other philosophical proponents have been so busy politicking to resolve the arguments in their favor, they have forgotten to further the field of education. In fact, the standards of teaching, teacher certification, and curriculum content are in the most deplorable condition they have ever been.

People who would have made great teachers have been discouraged by the low pay and dangerous working conditions in the field. Many teachers are not professionally equipped to teach their subjects in an ever changing world.

Worst of all, the so-called "educated" children of the last generation have for the most part been ill-prepared for the real world. Many of these young people can't even balance their own checkbooks, read simple contracts for renting apartments, or even purchase their own automobiles

They certainly have not been prepared for life.

When an employer tries to employ some of these functional illiterates, the first thing the employer must do is teach first grade reading, writing, and simple arithmetic. Meanwhile our schools have given these young people diplomas which state that the students have fulfilled the prescribed courses of study. Who are we to believe?

This has become a very competitive world and we as a nation are relying on our youth to carry us into the next century. Therefore our first priority is to reform the education system from top to bottom, and to prepare our young people for a globally competitive 21st century.

Language

According to the World Atlas:
the official language of France is French;
the official language of Germany is German;
the official language of Russia is Russian.

If you were to move to any one of those countries and enter your children in school they would be required to speak, read, write, and discuss in class *everything* in the language of that country.

In places like Canada and Belgium (among many others) the use of two languages have caused their people to go to the brink of civil war, because of the dispute over language.

The United States was founded as an English speaking nation and through wars and acquisitions such as the Louisiana Purchase and the Gadsden Purchase, (which firmed up the boundaries for the lower 48 states) the size of the continental portion of our country has remained the same for over 100 years, and all of our history, communications, and laws have been written and spoken in English.

It has only been these past 30 years, because of government and bureaucratic meddling, that we have begun teaching people with Hispanic surnames, in Spanish. Even though many Hispanic people have lived in this country for two or three generations or more, they are forced to put their children in classrooms with kids whose parents recently came to the United States.

The United States is an English speaking nation and we should insist on all students reading, writing, and speaking English.

English as a second language classes started out as a remedial program to get youngsters caught up to their peers in English not as a product unto itself. We must return to that policy as soon as possible.

We have seen millions of Asians who came from China, Japan, Vietnam, Thailand, Korea, and other places over the past 30 years and we haven't stopped to teach them in their native languages in our public schools — so why should we make a special case for Spanish?

It then follows that if we teach only English, then our ballots, driving tests, and everything else in our society should be in English.

In France, Germany, or even Mexico, everything is written in their native languages, as it rightly should be; the same goes for us.

The oldest problem on earth is that of communication. Many of the problems in our own country have come about in recent years from our failure to communicate with each other.

Gangs of youths have sprung up all over our country, many of whom speak in a variety of languages. Not only do these young gangsters speak vulgar colloquialisms, but unfortunately, our "good youngsters" are exposed to that poor language usage through television, rap music, and movies.

It is my opinion, that priority number one for our entire education system should be to ensure that every student receive a thorough education in speaking, reading, and writing of English before that student is permitted to move to the next grade level.

Minimum standards must be set and firmly adhered to.

I, for one, am embarrassed to listen to so-called college educated athletes being interviewed on radio or television. Many of these people can barely use 3rd or 4th grade vocabulary, and these are the role models for the youth to emulate?

I cringe when an athlete on a professional basketball or football team is introduced as former All-American from _____University, who played all four years on his college team. And then this person tries to answer simple questions asked by the reporter.

"Well, ya know ah," and then he bumbles a few words some more, "Ya know," and "Ya know," and "Ya know," come out with a few other well worn clichés.

I sure would hate to be the President of that man's university. Is that the kind of product our institutions of higher learning are turning out?

When we listen to the sit-coms or commercials on television, the same brand of street language is used to relate to a certain segment of the population.

How did those people get out of elementary or middle school? Who graded their papers?

Television and the movies are partly responsible for the poor English which is used. Between vulgar idioms and street talk, our impressionable youngsters learn all the incorrect ways of speaking and vocabulary usage. It makes one wonder if we are getting anyone to adhere to any English language standard.

In order to turn this all around, we are going to need the cooperation of parents, educators, media people, and the government. Everyone involved with children must begin by admitting that there is a language problem before we go about trying to solve it.

The solution is simple, just go back to teaching English as we did in the first 50 years of this century. Require students to read a certain amount of books per semester and have them submit book reports. The students should also write essays and do short reports on whatever interests them: vacations, sporting events, family get-togethers, or whatever, just so they begin to develop a writing style.

I have met high school and college graduates, over these many years who have bragged that they matriculated from their schools without ever having read one book. Some educational system! According to a much publicized survey, nearly 60 percent of all adult Americans never read one book, and the better part of the remaining 40 percent read no more than one book a year.[1]

Business and industry have been complaining for years that the education system of this country has been sending them functional illiterates, most of whom cannot be trained in the most simple of tasks.

It all begins with reading and writing correctly. We must have a national standard and we must begin by teaching our English language to our youth, and forget

---

[1] *The Death of Literature,* Alvin Kernan, New Haven, 1990

about second languages. We must communicate with each other before we can communicate with the rest of the world.

Discipline

When I began teaching in the 1950s, discipline was a minor problem. Every now and then, a youngster would get out of line, and the teacher would send the student to the principal or call in the parents for a conference to get the student back on track.

Today, schools (particularly high schools) have become armed camps. Monitors patrol the grounds with billy clubs and walkie-talkies, and teachers have to act like police first, to establish order, and then if there is any time left, they try to teach.

In an earlier chapter, I discussed the option of taking the trouble makers out of the classroom and sending them off to boys' and girls' towns which would be created from army camps.

The remaining youngsters must be taught from first grade on that they are expected to learn their subject matter in each course, and the failure to do so will result in the students repeating the grade. The business of passing children to the next grade level because of "good kidsmanship" must stop. It gives the students a false sense of security which will not hold up when they go out into the world. Many of these youngsters think that they have been educated by virtue of diplomas from elementary and high schools only to find out that in the real world they are unable to compete. If a company makes an inferior product, they will not be paid just because they are nice fellows. The product must pass the scrutiny of the buyer before the manufacturer is paid. We must consider our students our products. If they cannot perform the skills required, they should not be rewarded.

Nations such as Japan and Germany place a great deal of emphasis on discipline, and the students, are told that they are in a global conflict for economic survival. The U.S. is in no less a conflict, and if we come up lacking, the results could be catastrophic.

Things like forced busing haven't achieved anything but negative results. The children who are driven many miles to a strange neighborhood have no means of identity with that community. Their parents, who work hard all day, are not about to drive many miles for teachers' conferences or to attend school functions.

Moreover, the negative impact on most communities has been a phenomenon known as "White Flight." The moment the more financially affluent people were made aware that their local schools were mandated to bus in children from minority communities, they merely moved out to suburbs that didn't have busing. Some even put their children in private schools.

The results of forced busing have devastated some central districts of our largest cities because they lost the taxes paid by the more affluent people. After over 20 years of forced busing, the test scores of the children who were bussed, have remained the same — deplorable.

Americans do not like to have mandates forced down their throats, and busing has been one of the most reprehensible of those mandates.

We should give our attention and highest priorities to seeing that every child gets a well rounded education. Take the money used in busing and spend it on educating children.

In earlier years, when a student studied law, medicine, etc., it was said that he was taking up the *discipline* of law or *discipline* of medicine. This may be considered an outmoded use of the language, but the emphasis is correct. Learning is not possible without discipline.

Teachers of my acquaintance have told me that they are unable to motivate their students because most of the parents do not take an interest in their children's education.

I was a musician and music teacher for nearly ten years. In order to supplement my income, I would give private lessons. It was easy to see which children's parents showed an interest in their music.

When a parent sat down with his or her child while the child was practicing, that child progressed. When a youngster was sent into the next room to practice, rarely did that child ever go anywhere musically.

Great artists such as Jascha Heifitz and Anton Rubenstein, along with hundreds of other great performers, have related stories about how their mothers or fathers sat down with them and didn't let them go out and play until they finished their lessons.

There is rarely such a thing as a natural aptitude for practicing, studying, reading, or any other educational discipline. Children emulate their parents in practically everything they do.

If a parent is an alcoholic or drug user, the child for the most part, will grow up to be the same.

Conversely, if the child sees the parent taking an interest in his or her school work and praises the child for his or her accomplishments, usually the child will be a good student.

This is not a prescription for everyone being a straight "A" student or for being another Heifitz; it is merely a guideline for getting a child to learn his life skills by starting at an early age and being encouraged by the adults in his circle of family and friends.

We cannot show hypocrisy to our children. If they see parents reading and discussing literature, the children will want to also read and discuss what they read. If parents understand that children will follow their discipline, the children will also be disciplined.

Affirmative Action in Education

It is my experience that anything to do with education that does not have a bearing on the real world, tends to give the wrong signal to our youth.

How can we inject a quota system based on a population or other arbitrarily drawn criteria, and then have the children watch a college or professional football, baseball or basketball game on television, and see that the best athletes, regardless of color are playing on the team.

In real life, you put the best person on the team, not the one who follows some quota system.

My grandfathers both came to this country in the early 1900s and neither one knew one word of English, but they each raised families of *American* children and grandchildren, who were educated, and became worthwhile citizens. All of this without one penny of taxpayers' money to help them along the way.

They and millions of others who came to this country were given the opportunity to be what ever they wished to be, and to raise families in peace and freedom. None of those millions of people (many of whom came from totalitarian nations) were ever paid anything because of their terrible experiences.

Socialism is over! It has died the death that any poorly thought out social philosophy should die. It sank by its own weight of ineptitude and has left, in its wake, a few generations of lazy, unmotivated people.

One only has to see the problem in the former Soviet Union of people suddenly left on their own after "Big Brother" has gone away. It was made up of artificial prices supported by the state; cradle to the grave jobs, most of which were dead-end, make-work jobs; and a bankrupt political-economic system wherein a few elitist became fabulously wealthy while the average person barely eked out a living. This is the legacy of Socialism.

We also have seen the backside of Socialism — violence! When people are no longer getting a free ride, they turn to crime.

On paper Socialism sounds nice, but in practice it completely forgets human nature — namely to take the easy way out.

In order for our nation to maintain its leadership, we will need the talents and energy of all of our people. They must be well educated and able to use the communication tools and skills required in the 21st century. The next section will briefly propose the curriculum required to teach our students those skills.

Curriculum

We cannot presume to anticipate all of the requirements of the many school districts of this nation, however, we do know many subjects which must be taught properly, and many other subjects which I would like to see added to the curriculum.

We have seen recent questionnaires given to college students which show how uniformed they are about the history and geography of their own country. It goes without saying, that social studies must be taught to every student from at least the fourth grade up through the university level.

I remember that in the fifth grade of my elementary school in Chicago, we had a stamp club which was supervised by a very bright social studies teacher. By the end of the fifth grade, I knew every country in the world, capital cities, major products, the rivers, mountains, lakes, bays outside of the countries, and the major waterways.

Todays' kids couldn't even tell a questioner where Berlin or Moscow is located.

The history and politics of our nation are very important to every American, particularly around election time. I am amazed how little so-called educated people know about the workings of our nation.

In a recent poll, college students were asked how many justices there are in the Supreme Court. A minority could answer correctly (nine). Fewer knew anything about the electoral college, or how bills go through the government.

We teach English throughout the first eight grades and through much of high school, yet a large number of our young people go out into the world and are unable to read a simple lease when they rent their first apartment, and cannot understand the language written in a conditional sales contract for furniture or an automobile.

I would therefore suggest that sample leases, contracts, trust deeds, and the rest of the tools of our society be studied, at the very minimum at the high school curriculum.

It is also very important that our rich heritage of literature be required reading by all students from the fifth grade on through university. As I mentioned earlier, I have met high school and university graduates who boast about the fact that they never read a single book, outside of their textbooks, throughout their years of education.

Many parents never read to their children, or more importantly, children never see their parents reading.

Nevertheless, the school should not have to rely on the parents when it comes to the basic 3-R's; these children must be taught the discipline of reading, and they must be able to write their own book reports in correct English. As we mentioned before, unless we can communicate first with each other, and later on a national and global scale, we will fail as a nation.

Mathematics

In today's world, mathematical and computer skills are intertwined. Computers should be introduced into the curriculum by at least the junior high level (6th grade). In the early grades, it might be a practical exercise to "play" house which should include paying house or rent payments, purchasing groceries, automobile payments and expenses, utility bills, clothing, and other expenses.

The students should learn to use a checkbook, issue checks, and balance those checksbooks at the end of each month. This simple game of practical experience could start in the third or fourth grade, because then the students would be practicing simple addition and subtraction. This would give them a real-world application of the use of arithmetic.

In the higher grades, mathematics should be applied to other scientific problems such as figuring gasoline mileage or distances between U.S. cities and foreign capitals. By the end of high school, all students should have experienced the practical application of mathematics, not simply theories, and these programs should be updated regularly to take in the latest happenings worldwide.

Science

Nearly every day new breakthroughs happen in the many different fields of science. Medicine, chemistry, biology, and botany. Many of our students are studying from text books over 10 and 20 years old. In scientific terms, these texts are in the dark ages.

In order to stimulate and motivate our young people, we must bring the latest of everything into the classroom. This might mean having liaisons with the many scientific communities to bring in new discoveries, and even guest lecturers to speak about their latest discoveries.

More scientific knowledge was gained in the past 50 years than in the previous total history of man. There is nothing more boring than studying an outdated textbook, when common knowledge tells us that much of the information is obsolete.

Humanities

The entire sum of what makes up our civilization is recorded in our books, poetry, music, art, and theater. Just because ones' grandparents or parents attended art and musical events and read a great deal of literature, does not mean that the new generation has received those experiences through inheritance.

An education in the arts is an acquired education, but without a proper foundation in the humanities, our young people, if left to their devices, can easily revert to more primitive times.

We, as adults, must be ever vigilant to never permit our society to slack off, and thus wipe out many hundreds of years of culture.

Young children must observe their parents reading and discussing literature; they must be taken to classical music events, art shows, live theater and discussions about these events should include the children.

I don't expect young children to be able to sit through a four-hour Wagner opera, or a long classical concert. There are many children's concerts and opera performances in most cities which can be attended. Sometimes schools are invited to bring their students, but I am sure that if enough people showed interest in educating their children in music or theater arts, the local organizations would be more than happy to create extra performances to accommodate new, up-and-coming future patrons.

We must make our feelings known to our school administrators so that they might begin to reemphasize the humanities. There are certainly more than enough rock concerts to go around and for the most part, they have a negative educational value.

Many of these folk-rock heroes who were set up as role models turned out to be drug addicts and quite a few died long before their time. People such as Janis Joplin (died at age 27), Jimi Hendrix (died at age 27), Jim Morrison (died at age 26), John Beliushi (died at age 36), Elvis Presley (died at age 42), and the list goes on.

I have often heard young people say that they don't like classical music, they only like the rock and roll, rap, acid rock and all of the rest of the modern idioms. The only real retort is that how can one appreciate that which he has not studied, or been exposed to?

Long before a child enters school, parents can play simple recordings or tapes to their children, and most importantly, they can read to their kids. By deferring art, music, reading and theater to the schools and other children, learning the components of Western Civilization is never accomplished, and most children are left thereby impoverished.

When Jerry Garcia, the founder of the rock group The Grateful Dead passed away recently from too many years of drugs, many of his followers (who called themselves Deadheads, an appropriate name if I ever heard one) came out and said that the 1960s were over.

Where have they been for 30 years? Of course the 1960s are over, and so is most of the millennium over. The important statement should be, what have we learned from yesterday, and what are we going to do about it?

It pains me to see the level to which the so-called pop music has fallen.

When one enters a restaurant, or listens to a radio or television commercial, his senses are offended by the noise and objectionable racket which is supposed to pass for music. Since when does good music have to be loud?

Unfortunately, the schools, for the most part, have created the vacuum that has allowed this entire rock and rap culture to come about, simply because they have dropped music and music appreciation from most curriculums.

Even the high school bands that are left can barely play the national anthem, and the school fight song in tune.

And the loud, brash and raucous street music that has taken the place of good music has become a subculture in this nation. The license to wear crazy clothes, dye hair purple, green and other weird colors; wear makeup, (some of which resembles stone age tribes); and use liquor and drugs, resort to violence and have illegitimate children, displays the antisocial behavior that has been the terrible legacy of this so-called rebellion.

When the space shuttle Discovery was in orbit, the space center in Houston played the song Beautiful Ohio as a "wake up" song because most of the crew was from

Ohio. One television station decided to have a "man on the street" program to ask young people if they liked that song. Not one person interviewed had ever even heard "Beautiful Ohio."

I wonder what kind of answers they would give to Rhapsody in Blue or Swan Lake?

In order to have culture, we must teach culture. This is not to mean that we expect all of our children to be professional musicians or artists. We, as a civilized society, must pass along those things that make us a civilized society.

You never hear about a riot breaking out in a symphony concert, opera, or art showing. Rock concerts seem to bring out the beast in our young people. Shootings, stabbings, looting, drunkenness, drug usage, rapes and other criminal behavior usually emanates from the attendance of young, immature youngsters who get "turned on" by the wild and provocative jungle music.

Unless we expose the young people to the best of our culture, we can expect the next generation to turn out even more rebellious than the present generation.

Physical Education

The YMCA, of which I was privileged to be a local board member, and later president, has a slogan which is "Mind, Body and Spirit" all three elements which are necessary to make well-rounded citizens. In the 20th Century, athletics has been overemphasized to the exclusion of educating young people.

The entire student body, teachers, administrators, parents and friends show up each week to watch 30 to

40 football players or 5 to 15 basketball players perform. The audience is passive while just a handful participate.

The YMCA method is to allow everyone to participate. When the basketball game is on the line in the last minute of play, the youngster who hasn't played gets on the court. The emphasis is on learning how to compete, not how to win at any price.

The lessons now being taught in our schools and universities is that winning is everything. We deify kids who can't read or write, but are able to block, tackle, run, score, pass, or shoot baskets, and this tends to diminish the efforts of the best students.

Every once in a while we hear of a good student, who is also a good athlete, but in the main, athletic prowess comes first.

This prevailing attitude regarding winning at all costs carries on in the universities where athletes are wooed by the largest schools and are given scholarships, free room and board, and any number of perks, most of which are rarely made public.

The outstanding students, on the other hand, must fend for themselves. There is an occasional tuition scholarship given to a few outstanding students, but mostly, these students are left to their own devices and family support to get through school.

After graduation (or in most athlete's cases, when they have played out their 4 years of eligibility, or sooner if they are superstars), some of these athletes are signed to professional contracts which pay enormous bonuses, salaries, and perks, while the great students have to start at the bottom rung of their chosen field, and spend a lifetime getting to the top. They will, for the most part, never earn the millions of dollars paid their athletic schoolmates.

The great athletes, many of whom never graduate or even satisfactorily pass any solid academic courses, turn professional and start out earning astronomical wages.

I recently heard of a young man who was paid $7 million just to sign a contract and was guaranteed $30 million for his first five years of play. There are all kinds of million dollar bonus deals given to young men who haven't played a single down, or a single inning, or shot a single basket in professional ball. (Most of these athletes earn more money in one year than the entire payroll of the average public elementary school.)

What kind of a value statement is that sending to our youth? All you have to do is be a super jock, and to hell with school? All of those hard-working students who legitimately pass all of their courses of study, matriculate through university and start at the bottom rung of the ladder do not make such great role models when compared to the athletes who, for the most part, take easy courses and never legitimately graduate from any high school or university just because they are capable of bringing some fame and glory to their schools.

The Gaming Industry

When I was a young man, gambling was considered a vice, not to be participated in by nice boys and girls. The real world, however, was quite different.

I could remember the football cards being passed around in the playground. The cards would show 10 or

12 games being played this coming weekend and the idea of winning the gamble was to pick several winners. I never knew the odds or what money you would win for your quarter, but the cards were out there for grammar-school aged kids, and they were always available in high school and college.

I was too busy with my school work and musical activities to pay much attention to what was going on in this minor underworld, but throughout the ensuing years, these cards were distributed all over the nation, and into every possible kind of situation. Cards were available in industrial plants, health clubs, country clubs, and for every conceivable age and economic strata.

In fact the entire gambling industry, (now called by the Newspeak term of Gaming Industry) is the second largest industry in the United States, next only to the government itself. Gambling is estimated to be a $500 billion annual business.

Places such as Las Vegas, Reno, Atlantic City, and many other major and minor gambling meccas, along with the ever-present lotteries, horse-racing tracks, and all of the steamboats and, cruise vessels, have given the mobsters who are the main beneficiaries of the sins of gambling, a new status of elitism.

There are jingles on the television and radio extolling the "easy" way to get your dream house, or great riches or the latest dreams being pitched. All the while, our young people must be thinking that having to go to school and struggle to get to the top is a sucker's game when you just have to buy the winning ticket or spin the big wheel.

How can a nation, which throws a ½ trillion dollars away each year on gambling not have the capability of hiring the finest teachers, building the best schools and giving our kids the best education in the world? We are going to have to rearrange and prioritize where we spend our money.

Gambling is another form of corruption — no different than drugs or prostitution, only it is being committed by otherwise, legitimate people.

Early in this book, I spoke of the analogy of the decline and fall of the Roman Empire, and the decline of our nation as we know it.

The gladiators were used by the Roman Emperors and other leaders to give their people pride in place of the real substance of a decent standard of living and a foundation of learning and education. The gladiators were the opiate of the Roman society.

In other words, the gladiators, just like our own high school, university, and professional athletes are merely window dressings to obscure the view of what is really going on, namely the disintegration of our society.

In the early days of our nation, we did not need sporting events to take the place of our personal and family goals. The high-powered hype and promotion of big time school and professional sports really began in the 1950s when after a very frustrating Korean War, we found that a saddened and disillusioned country needed artificial stimuli to feel good about itself. Athletics and wild music has filled that void, and we have unhappily seen the results.

The "win-at-any-cost" syndrome has caused many of our young athletes to turn to drugs, liquor, and wild life styles. Many of these young people have died or been crippled for life, when for many, life has just begun. And these overpaid, over pampered, uneducated, inarticulate people have unfortunately become the role models for our youth. One radio talk show features the "athlete arrest of the day." (A sarcasm, which aptly states the revulsion many people have to this out-of-control system.)

This entire process of emphasizing athletics must be rolled back if we are to develop the next generation into worthwhile and productive citizens. The very idea that you do not have to do your homework, attend classes, or get decent grades, has got to be stopped. This may not be a very popular idea in many quarters, but I must remind the reader that this book is about Re-Civilizing America, not perpetuating its sacred cows.

If education is going to be worth its place in America, it is going to have to educate all of its people. I have seen cases of young men in their 30s after finishing a career in professional sports, having earned (and spent) millions of dollars, unable to support themselves and their families by the most menial of jobs. There is something wrong, and we must fix it now.

Marriage and the Family

Every high school in this nation should teach a course of study in how to select a husband or wife; how to be a good husband or wife; and how to be a good parent.

We have, for too long, relied on the hope that all of us instinctively will be good family people because we all come from good families. If that were really true, how come the divorce rate is so high? Why are there so many abused spouses and abused children? Why have so many teenaged pregnancies occurred? Why are these young mothers and their children abandoned by their fathers? (In 1993, 22% of all white children born and 73% of all black children born, were illegitimate.)

Who is responsible for this whole mess? The answer, as we earlier stated, is we the people. We have not spent enough time raising our children to be responsible citizens, spouses and parents. Therefore the law of the jungle prevails — everyone is for himself.

Parents, of course, have a personal stake in what happens to their children, but with both parents often working and, as we also said earlier, since many of them also come from broken homes and abusing parents, it falls entirely on the education system to teach young people the civilized way to form and raise a family.

By no means, does this mean to bring religion into the classroom. It does, however, mean that our western society has existed for hundreds of years with a solid moral code, which if understood by administrators, and reaches parents, and students, can go far in developing a proper foundation for the teaching of marriage and the family.

Other Courses in the Curriculum

I have not purposely left out courses in language, business, economics, or other important learning tools that we have developed over the years, but I have found that if these courses are made available to all students, that some of them may be eagerly taken and others may not, depending upon the interests of the students.

The leadership of educators to keep our nation from falling into another Dark Age, cannot be emphasized enough. The challenge which faces our very dedicated teachers and administrators is awesome, but the American spirit of "can do" must be able to overcome that challenge lest we fall into an irreversible abyss.

> *Nations are destroyed, or flourished,*
> *in proportion as their poetry, painting,*
> *and music are destroyed or flourished.*
> *—William Blake (1757-1827)*

TAKING OUR COUNTRY BACK

Illegal Immigration

In these past years of liberal permissiveness, we have allowed millions of immigrants into our country; most of whom came in illegally, and many others who were given special permission by Congress, the President, or both.

I do not believe in an isolationist "America for the Americans" policy. We are a nation of immigrants who were allowed into this country in an orderly, legal way, and America's greatness came about because of these new people who had ambitions and dreams, and were permitted by a free nation to go as far as their abilities permitted.

In recent years, our immigration policy has become a disaster. When Cuba's President Castro let thousands of people out of prisons and mental institutions, we permitted those misfits into our country. The crime rate in Florida (and other places where these refugees settled) went into orbit. Peaceful retirement cities such as Miami have turned into jungles. Robberies, car thefts, drug dealings, rapes, drive-by shootings, and all of the other tawdry statistics have been visited upon formerly peaceful communities.

Several hundred thousand Vietnamese were similarly permitted into this country without proper physical or criminal background checks, and places such as Orange County, California, have seen gang warfare on a scale never before witnessed. Young criminals extort money from merchants, and other individuals, and if the victims do not pay up, they usually lose their lives. People's homes are being broken into while they are home, and family members are robbed, raped, assaulted, and most of these gang members get off scott free because their victims fear reprisals.

There are an estimated 1 million Vietnamese in California alone.

The southern borders of our nation have been overwhelmed these past 25 years by people not only from Mexico, but also by many thousands of illegals from Central America. It is estimated that over 500,000 Salvadorans now live in California. All of these people had to *walk* from their towns and villages to our country, a distance farther than that from New York to California.

The crime rates have been on the rise in proportion to all of the these new illegals in our country. The most alarming statistic of all, is that the minute most of these people cross our boarders, they sign up for welfare, subsidized housing, hospital and medical assistance, food stamps and all of the rest of the free help they can get — all at the expense of the hard working American Citizen. They enroll their children in our schools, and then look for employment, usually in the underground economy. Most of these immigrants become gardeners, busboys, dishwashers, day laborers or other service jobs where they usually are paid in cash. The women get employment as housemaids, hotel maids, seamstresses in the garment factories, and waitresses and they also are paid in cash.

No income taxes or social security taxes are paid by the overwhelming majority of these people, yet they continue to collect welfare, food stamps and the other benefits listed above.

Our policy towards these immigrants must change, and change soon, lest we sink by the sheer weight of their needs.

One remedy I spoke of in Chapter 3 of this book is to get rid of the income tax and invoke a value-added sales tax. This would, in some measure, force these immigrants to pay their fair share of running the country, state, and city governments.

Secondly, we must stop *all* welfare and other giveaways to all illegal people. Nobody supported our grandparents and parents when they came to America; therefore why should the latest wave of people, who didn't even arrive legally, be given the red carpet treatment?

Finally, we must tighten up our borders and only admit people who meet the normal qualifications to become legal citizens of this country.

Elections

A great deal of this book has to do with politicians, bureaucrats and influence peddlers. It has been through political chicanery that our country is in its present mess.

A movement which has been a long time in coming is term limits of politicians. That sounds like a high-minded idea, but in most places with political machines such as Chicago, New York, Detroit, and Kansas City, the proposal will never fly as long as the political machine is in power and can promote its candidates from its own ranks.

These machines must be broken up and left in the ashes of history. We citizens must not look for the easy fix every time we come to an impasse. The stranglehold machine politicians have upon their constituencies are the *favors* they have granted over the years. The clever politicians have people *owing* them for the favors, large and small, rendered over the years. They collect their dues on election day.

Election reform must go hand and hand with a knowledgeable electorate. We have let "George" do it for too long; now it is time that we elect only those people who will be accountable to We The People. It is very important that we attend forums run by independent groups to hear all candidates speak, and it is equally important to ask questions about the candidate's positions on matters which concern us. If we do not take a personal interest in what is happening in our community, city, county, state or federal levels, we will keep on getting the same business as usual representation that we have been burdened with in the past.

My idea of election reform is that a candidate would not be able to run for any other office after his two terms are up. He (or she) would have to stay out of office for four years before being permitted to run for any office except the one in which he has already served.

This way, we would not have the same cast of characters changing hats with each other.

We must also limit the time a candidate starts to run for political office. Some candidates begin collecting funds, and plotting the next campaign, the day after they are sworn into office.

Lobbyists and influence peddlers play a large part in the running of government. We have former Congressmen and Senators in the employ of foreign governments, labor unions, racket bosses and thousand of other pressure groups. The selling-out of the American people must stop, or we are on the same course as ancient Rome: annihilation.

As citizens, we must insist on fair and honest dealings from our elected officials. The graft and corruption which now exists must be eliminated so that our country is not driven into bankruptcy, and our people impoverished by ambitious and greedy politicians, and criminals.

The United States has come to be known as an unsafe place to visit, most particularly, in our large cities. To our everlasting shame, many visitors to our shores have been murdered, assaulted, robbed and otherwise scared enough to never want to visit America again.

As stated earlier, there are not enough police to cover all of the crimes which are perpetrated daily; so what is the solution?

Part of our solution is to say what we mean about law enforcement, and then mean what we say about punishment of criminals. Many young hooligans who are caught dealing in drugs, stealing cars, committing rapes, are usually given light sentences either because they are first time offenders or because they are young and should be given another chance.

Wrong, Wrong, Wrong!!!

Usually when a so-called first time offender is brought before a bar of justice, he is very well practiced in his trade of crime he may just have been *caught* as if for the first time.

By letting such an individual off with a light sentence, allows this person to show-off to his peers that he has "beaten the system," and become a hero.

Countries such as Turkey, Saudi Arabia have instant, cruel punishment for drug dealers. They chop off their heads. No leniency, no second chance, nothing. I do not believe in such cruel, inhuman methods of punishment, but I do believe that our lenient criminal justice system can learn something from those barbaric methods.

If a young criminal is sent right to prison and is made to serve several years of hard time, his peers might think twice about committing crimes.

No plea bargains, and no bleeding hearts. These young criminals are the products of their families upbringing — they were allowed to run the streets and get into mischief at early ages; they were allowed to be antisocial in school; and now, at the eleventh hour they expect society to be lenient?

Justice must be swift and consistent. When gangs of young people decide to burn down neighborhoods in Detroit, Michigan, every year at Halloween night because it has become a tradition, the Governor of Michigan or the mayor of Detroit should declare martial law and shoot the burners and looters on sight. This would stop that sort of "tradition" in its tracks.

Many of our urban neighborhoods have drug dealings going on every night, and people are afraid to be on the streets. These nests of drug dealers could be cleaned out by calling out the National Guard, and equipping them with riot gear and sweeping through those neighborhoods, to clean house once and for all.

After declining steadily through the 1980s, teenage drug use, especially of marijuana, has jumped sharply. Daily use among eight-graders has *quadrupled* since 1992, according to University of Michigan's Institute for Social Research.

In a recent survey of 12 to 17 year olds, more than half said heroin and cocaine were readily available.

The youthful drug epidemic is further fueled through popular culture, especially rock music. At the Lollapalooza music festival July of 1995 in Great Woods, Massachusetts, the mostly white, suburban teen crowd cheered wildly when rap group Cypress Hill pushed a six-foot-tall *bong,* or water pipe, on stage. The group has sold five million copies of its first two albums, one of which included songs titled "Legalize it," "Hits From the Bong" and "I wanna Get High."

Popular rock star Tom Petty regularly glamorizes marijuana use in concerts and songs. Petty's latest top-selling album includes the lyrics "Let's get to the point. Let's roll another joint." In another he sings, "It's good to get high and never come down."

The penalty for drug dealing should be life in prison without any chance of parole. If we intend to clean up our nation we must resolve to *clean* it completely.

Once these young people see that there is no longer a weak or soft approach to crime, and that we as a society mean business, these youngsters might rethink beginning a life of crime.

If one is found guilty of murder, then he or she should be executed within a reasonable time. Some criminals wait on death row for 10 or 15 or 20 years while their lawyers make a mockery of justice. All the while the families and friends of the victims wait for justice to be carried out.

Industry

We must get rid of the rules and regulations promulgated these past 30 years which only served to drive industry and business out of our country. Tax laws such as a luxury tax on boats and cruisers, which all but destroyed the boat building industry in this country, are counter productive and should be rescinded immediately.

The boat builders in the Caribbean Islands and other places had a field day when our Congress enacted the 20% tax, but we also lost thousands of jobs and the income taxes which could have been derived from those jobs.

The whole idea that the Federal or State Governments are capable of macro-managing the economy, has come to mean, that by bureaucratic bungling, we have lost thousands of industries and millions of jobs.

Where are those jobs today? Mostly in Asia. Countries such as China, Japan, Singapore, Taiwan, Korea, Thailand, and others are rolling in American dollars. These countries have none of our strict environmental, or tax laws, but they sure have the jobs and the bucks.

American industrial and entrepreneurial skills do not take a back seat to anyone in the world, provided they can compete on a level playing field. The restrictive rules, laws, taxes and all the rest should be immediately rescinded so that American industry can once again compete in the world marketplace.

I remember during the 1960s and 1970s when many of our people were purchasing Volkswagens, Toyotas, or any number of other foreign automobiles, and then boasting about how they were able to get superior gas mileage over American products. I wonder how many of those people who used to park their foreign autos in their company parking lots are reflecting on those purchases now that their company parking lots are vacant, and so are the company buildings?

We are an inter-related economy. If we lose jobs in one place, then those wage earners can no longer purchase products which are made in another place.

By purchasing foreign products over American products, we have undermined our entire financial stability as a nation. Just recently, Zenith, the last television made in the U.S. was purchased by a foreign corporation. Several years ago, a U.S. Senator exclaimed that "one day we will be a nation of television repairmen." We are headed in that direction.

Between Mr. Nader's convincing the public time and time again that they are being "ripped off" by American industry, and the heavy taxes and rules imposed by our bureaucrats, our industry is on the proverbial ropes.

Many industrial leaders have repeatedly said that the heavy burden put upon our manufacturers makes it nearly impossible to do business, and compete in a global market.

Very little of this matters to our swivel chair bureaucrats. They receive their salaries every week, they get their paid vacations every year, they have wonderful medical benefits for themselves and their families, and their pension programs are all secured. Why should they care if business and industry are suffering?

We have taken the American dream and turned it into an Orwellian nightmare.

American business is run mostly by Americans, and their employees are our neighbors and friends. To vilify our business as being "rip off" artists is not only unconscionable, it is un-American. Mr. Nader and the rest of his ilk, in conjunction and full cooperation of our elected officials and their appointed stooges, have caused irreparable harm to our nation.

Every year we have a negative trade balance in the $100 billion plus range, and our worldwide competitors have a good laugh at the stupidity of the American government.

I would recommend that a blue ribbon committee made up of industry representatives, unions, government experts and people from the academic community convene, and lay down a new plan to save American business. The time for name calling is past we are in survival mode, and must be willing to take extreme measures to put our manufacturers back on their feet.

Once we have executed these plans, we must get rid of the government bureaus, and the red tape that they have forced on American industry. In other words, we need a new "Marshall Plan" to save American business.

The next World War will be fought with computers and bank balances. We must get our manufacturing and business communities healthy, and soon, or we are lost.

Population

The population of the United States in 1940, at the start of World War II, was 130 million. This means that from the time the Pilgrims landed in 1620, until 1940 (320 years) we reached the population of 130 million.

Since 1940, our population has doubled, in a short 56 years, to 260 million.[2] If we keep on this same course, we could have a population of 350 million to 500 million by the year 2050, 54 years from now. I don't think that we have either the industrial means or food resources to support a population that large.

For the last century we have watched nations such as China and India struggle with the terrible problems of overpopulation, and I am sure, that even though we sympathized with their plight, we could never envision such a catastrophe befalling the United States. Well, a half a

---

[2] Source: Bureau of Census, 1994

billion population is only 50 or 60 years away, and we have never heard any of our leaders mentioning this.

In order to keep our nation from returning to an agrarian age, where everyone will be forced to raise his or her own food, and make their own clothes, we are going to have to invoke a national policy of controlling the number of children a family should have. Religious considerations notwithstanding, we must voice the alarm now, not when the countries population is 350 to 400 million people. By that time, it will be too late.

The concept of zero population means that a couple would only be allowed two children. In other words, they could reproduce themselves. Families who have three or more children would be responsible for putting a negative burden on our country, and they should be discouraged, in the strongest terms, from having such large families.

In China, couples are punished if they have more than one child because that nation is extremely overpopulated. This must serve as a warning to our country as to what additional governmental interference can occur.

We could begin a population restraint program as early as junior or senior high school by illustrating the problems of overpopulation to students, long before they find a mate and decide to procreate. Biology classes should teach the concept of birth control, so that our young people can understand that having babies is not necessarily the natural outcome of marriage.

I am sure that people with very strong religious beliefs may take exception to this position. Just to dismiss this argument by saying that having many children is

"Gods will," won't solve the problem when we are over-populated, and cannot support our own people.

The argument of predicted overpopulation in a few short years, gives even greater justification for us to restrict immigration into our nation.

Never in the history of this country have we faced a population crisis such as we will face in the next century, and the time to take preventive measures is now.

Divide and Conquer

We have discussed in Chapter 8 the hate and divisive groups that have been put together to emphasize our differences.

I agree that men will never be women, nor will women ever be men, but do we have to dislike each other for having been born a different gender?

Black people will never be white, and white people will never be black, but we must learn to live with each other.

Young people will someday be old, and old people were once young, and each group must respect the other.

We are all Americans with a proud heritage and a brilliant future unless we destroy our nation by fighting with each other.

We must get rid of the guns, and disarm the militant groups who can only do harm to our nation with their inflammatory rhetoric, and then begin teaching our people to get along.

The movie and television industries could go a long way in helping solidify America by developing family value projects versus the mad, insane violence they now display. Young minds are very impressionable, and if they see our people depicted as murderous, violent, oversexed, and aberrant, then they "act out" the behavior they see on the screen.

The whole point of re-civilizing America is to teach our children the correct way to behave. This must be reflected at all levels. Parents, teachers, schools, family members, family friends, and everyone else, must comport themselves in a civil way, before we can expect civility from our children.

Those young people who are unable to conform with the standards of civilization must be removed from ordinary society to special schools and taught how to live and learn in a civilized manner.

It might take 20 years, or more, to raise a couple of generations of young people, but if we show a national resolve, these youngsters will grow up and be worthwhile citizens and their children will also be good citizens. This is the only way we can break the gang cycle.

Money

According to the Department of the Treasury, there are many hundreds of billions of dollars of "missing and unaccounted" money located both in this country and around the world. Additionally, there has been counterfeiting of American money, particularly in Iran and other Middle Eastern countries.

It is therefore of primary importance that the U.S. Treasury calls in all the outstanding money and exchanges it for new, "fool-proof" money.

You cannot bring prosperity by discouraging thrift.
You cannot strengthen the weak by weakening
the strong. You cannot help the wage earner by
pulling down the wage payer. You cannot further the
brotherhood of man by encouraging class hatred.
You cannot build character and courage by taking
away man's initiative and independence. You cannot
help men permanently by doing for them what
they could and should do for themselves.
—Abraham Lincoln

CONCLUSION

"If you want a picture of the future, imagine a boot stomping on a human face, forever."
1984 *by George Orwell*

In 1948, George Orwell wrote *1984*. He used the latter date as a transposition of the last two numbers of 48. This was a chilling story of a mythical country called Oceania (a thin disguise for England), which was ruled by an oppressive Big Brother, and which demanded complete control of people's lives, and minds.

Among the many inventions of Mr. Orwell was a language he called "Newspeak," which had been devised to meet the needs of Ingsoc, or English Socialism. The hero, Winston Smith, was a former journalist whose new job was rewriting history, including that of removing names from newspapers, books, which had fallen from favor with Big Brother.

In today's reality of more powerful government than the writers of our Constitution ever envisioned, coupled with high speed computers and other information gathering machines, we citizens are living in a fishbowl, not unlike the citizens of mythical Oceania. If we do something as simple as withdraw $10,000 from our bank account, the bank is obligated to inform the Internal Revenue Service. We have many other governmental rules and regulations which, in each case, have impuned our lives as free citizens. The list is too lengthy to enumerate. Suffice it to say, that the days of Big Brother have substantially lengthened, and our days as free Americans are greatly shortened.

Examples of Newspeak are things like President Kennedy's, New Frontier and President Johnson's, Great Society, both of which are Socialism with a new wrapper; Friendly Fire, which means that our soldiers are shot by their own comrades and Downsizing of industry, which means that people are fired or laid off from their jobs.

We have already discussed how people can pay into social security their whole working lives, only to have their contributions confiscated by the government if they should die before they reach 65 years of age.

Under our present rules, a person can work his whole life, pay taxes, and develop a large estate through hard work and disciplined savings, and then upon his death, the government taxes his estate, often wiping out his heirs. This is not only unfair, it is double taxation. We must get rid of inheritance taxes.

We as citizens have been conditioned to live in fear of the government, its agencies, and its awesome police powers.

This must stop, and stop now lest we become a totalitarian state as is described in 1984.

The bureaus and agencies of government must be closed if they do not serve any useful purpose beyond power and control. The Congress has put these agencies up as a buffer against having to answer to their constituencies. If you don't believe me, write to your Congressman about some problem you are having with a government agency. What you will probably get is a polite letter written by a secretary in the Congressman's office informing you that your letter was forwarded to the agency in charge of these matters.

This is hardly the representative form of government outlined in our Constitution, and executed the first 150 years of our nation's existence.

There would be plenty of money to educate our children, regain our families' pride, and live a high standard of life if we didn't have to waste most of our money on running a wasteful and mismanaged government.

The first and most important step we must take is to use the ballot box wisely. Politicians can be voted out of office just as easily as they were voted into office.

Our citizens have to exercise their franchise and vote in local and national elections, and put people into office who will follow the will of the people. The last several Presidential elections only had 50% of our citizens even turn out and vote.

As long as we think that we cannot change the system, the political machines, influence peddlers, politicians, bureaucrats and their legions of followers will have their way, and we will continue to get the form of Big Brotherism we do not need.

The opportunity to take back our country is now. We must show an interest in America. The alternative is unacceptable.

Presidents Reagan and Bush spoke many times about volunteerism to substitute for the myriad of government bureaus which take large amounts of money and then proceed to run our lives, but they never really amplified upon what they meant.

We Americans have shown to ourselves and to the rest of the world that we are a resourceful and generous people until we were shown an easy way out — government agencies to pick up the responsibilities of taking care of the less advantaged among us. Human nature being what it is, we thought that since the agencies were carrying out their duties, there really was no need for the rank and file Americans to get in the way.

We have learned the hard, and costly way that when we leave things to others, the tasks are done poorly. Moreover, as we previously mentioned, when people are given the free ride of welfare, food stamps, subsidized housing and all of the rest of the giveaways, they lose their incentives to go out and work for a living.

The mobilization I call for is that all able-bodied Americans go back to those things that made our country great — giving of themselves.

Institutions such as the American Red Cross, YMCA, Boys/Girls Clubs, Boy/Girl Scouts, Goodwill Industries, Salvation Army, Big Brothers/Big Sisters, Hospitals, Hospices, American Cancer Society, local Churches and Synagogues, would be delighted if we just called them up or went into their offices and volunteered our services.

Some people have special skills to offer such as typing or running a computer; others might be available to drive children or patients; still others just provide the man and women power needed to just take care of the daily tasks of running these volunteer organizations.

I for one, can attest to the great feeling I got from serving my fellow man. The many years I served the YMCA taught me a great deal about life I never would have read about in books or seen over television. A person grows as an individual when he or she serves and the community is better for it.

The organizations mentioned above and thousands of other services organizations need the *personal* help of every citizen who is willing to step in and do a service. The exemplary service of former President Jimmy Carter wielding a hammer to help provide housing for the needy should serve as a beacon to inspire us all to help our fellow countrymen and women.

The people of Rome didn't know what hit them when their nation collapsed because of the graft and corruption.

Let this be a warning to all Americans — we do not need to enter a dark age and be a footnote to history. We can mobilize and make our own history.

We must take back our country, rebuild our industries, educate and civilize our youth, and be forever on guard that we never let our nation be taken away from us again by people who only live for their own agendas.

America is the finest place on earth; let us be determined to keep it that way.

Eternal vigilance is the price of liberty.
—Thomas Jefferson